P9-BYU-235

Raising
a Princess

JOHN
CROYLE

B&H
PUBLISHING GROUP
Nashville, Tennessee

Copyright © 2014 by Big Oak Ranch, Inc.
All rights reserved.
Printed in the United States of America

978-1-4336-8073-1

Published by B&H Publishing Group
Nashville, Tennessee

Dewey Decimal Classification: 306.874
Subject Heading: VIRTUE \ CHILD REARING \
DAUGHTERS

Unless otherwise stated all Scripture is taken from
the ESV® Bible (The Holy Bible, English Standard Version®)
copyright © 2001 by Crossway Bibles,
a publishing ministry of Good News Publishers.
ESV® Text Edition: 2007. All rights reserved.

Also used: New American Standard Bible (NASB), © the
Lockman Foundation, 1960, 1962, 1963, 1968, 1971, 1972,
1973, 1975, 1977, used by permission.

Also used: New King James Version (NKJV), copyright ©
1979, 1980, 1982, Thomas Nelson, Inc., Publishers.

Also used: New International Version (NIV), Copyright ©
1973, 1978, 1984, 2011 by Biblica, Inc.® Used by permission.
All rights reserved worldwide.

1 2 3 4 5 6 7 8 • 18 17 16 15 14

I've made a lot of mistakes as a man, husband, and father; perhaps you have too. There came a time in my life when I decided to draw a line in the sand and grow up. Thankfully, it's never too late for any of us to change.

This book is dedicated to my princess, Reagan.
You changed my life forever.

Acknowledgments

To ALL the girls who have called Big Oak Ranch their home, who have taught all of us much more than we ever taught them.

This book is the culmination of countless hours that our frontline warriors, the houseparents at Big Oak Ranch, and our support staff have put into our "daughters" to mold them into the quality young ladies who will one day be somebody's queen.

Contents

Introduction

In 1985, I met a twelve-year-old girl named Shelley. Shelley had suffered the most unimaginable abuse at the hands of her parents and had been living in foster care for months. But now, the judge had decided it was time for her to be reunited with her family.

I pleaded with the judge not to send Shelley back into that situation. "If you make her go back to those people, she'll be dead in six months," I told him. At the time, Big Oak Ranch was a home for boys only. So I begged the judge to let Shelley come live with my wife Tee and me and our two little children. Anything to keep her out of her horrific situation at home.

But the judge wasn't moved by my pleading. For reasons I still don't understand, he sent Shelley back to her parents.

As it turned out, I was wrong in my prediction that Shelley would be dead in six months. She was beaten to death by her father three months later.

As we grieved Shelley's senseless death, Tee and I began praying about how we could help prevent this same thing from happening to other girls. That was the beginning of Big Oak Girls' Ranch.

We started the Boys' Ranch shortly after I graduated from the University of Alabama in 1974. In 1988 we opened the Girls' Ranch, thirty-five miles away. When you drive up to the Girls' Ranch from the main road, you're traveling on Shelley Drive. It's a daily reminder of why we do what we do.

Big Oak Ranch is a Christian home for children needing a chance. Our kids live in houses that probably look a lot like your house, in a neighborhood that looks more like a suburban subdivision than a "campus." They have house-parents whom they most of the time call "Mom" and "Dad." Hundreds of girls have lived at Big Oak Ranch since 1988. We have seen them through every imaginable parenting situation, from learning to ride a bike to going on a first date to heading off to college. (As I write this, twenty-one of our children are currently in college; almost all of them are the first from their family to go to college.)

I don't claim to have all the answers when it comes to raising daughters. I only claim to have a lot of experience, having had a part in the raising of every girl who has come through Big Oak Ranch since 1988.

Princess Power

Most of the girls at Big Oak Ranch have come out of unimaginable situations, many of them as bad as Shelley's. For the majority of these girls, their trust muscles are shredded, their self-image is destroyed, and their whole sense of how the world works is completely skewed—through no fault of their own.

I can tell some outrageous stories about the way parents have abused and mistreated their daughters—stories that I have experienced firsthand. I will, in fact, tell a few of those stories in the course of this book, though they only represent the tip of the iceberg of what I've seen and heard in my years at Big Oak Ranch. (I should point out, by the way, that in most of those stories I have changed names and identifying details.)

But of all the things these girls' parents did to them, the worst, I believe, was giving them the impression that nobody in the world cared about them or valued them. Girls come to Big Oak Ranch not understanding that they are princesses, created by God and valued by people who love them. Our first job—our main job—when raising these girls is to build up their sense that they are indeed as valuable and lovely as any other girl in the world. The girls at Big Oak Ranch are princesses of God.

And so is your girl.

If you're reading this book, you're probably not a parent who beats your daughter or burns her with cigarettes. You're probably not locking her in closets or neglecting to meet her physical needs. But does your daughter understand that she's a princess? Does she know that she is valued and as lovely as any other girl in the world? I see plenty of girls from good families who go to good schools and seem to have every advantage who think like orphans, not understanding who they are or *whose* they are because they aren't quite convinced that they are princesses or don't quite know what it would mean if they were.

This is a book about raising your daughter as a princess who knows exactly who God made her to be, even if she's not quite there yet.

The Princess and the Pea

I love the old fairy tale of "The Princess and the Pea." I also kind of hate it. You probably know this story already. There's a prince who looks everywhere for a princess to marry, but every girl he meets either isn't a princess or else, if she is a princess, she has some issue that keeps her from being a suitable mate. Then, one stormy night, a girl dressed in rags knocks on the castle door and asks for shelter for the night.

This bedraggled girl claims to be a princess. But she doesn't look like one, with her ragged clothing and wet, ratty hair. Still, there's something about her that the prince likes, and he hopes that she truly is a princess as she claims. So he creates a test: he piles twenty mattresses on the visitor's bed, and then places a pea under the bottom mattress. If the girl is a true princess, he reasons, she will be sensitive enough to feel the little pea through twenty mattresses.

The next morning, the prince asks the visitor how she slept. "Terrible," she says. "There was a lump in the bed that kept me from sleeping. It bruised me all over."

The prince knew that he had found a true princess. Who but a princess would be so sensitive that she would be bothered by a pea under twenty mattresses?

So, what do I love about that fairy tale? I love the idea that a princess is a princess no matter what her external circumstances. There are a lot of bedraggled, storm-tossed girls who show up at our door, who don't look like princesses at first glance. They don't believe themselves that they are princesses. But their royalty is there, just below the surface. It is the great joy of my life and of everybody at Big Oak Ranch to help those girls see that they are princesses.

And what do I hate about that fairy tale? I hate the idea that the essence of princess-hood is a finicky, persnickety sensitivity to the discomforts of real life. A princess, according to "The Princess and the Pea," is a girl who is used to being pampered, a girl who complains if things aren't exactly to her liking.

That's not my definition of a princess. A princess is a girl who knows she's a beloved daughter of the King. Because she understands that, she doesn't look to the world to tell her who she is. She doesn't listen to the world when it tells her, "Here's what you have to do if you want to be loved." She knows she's already loved.

So forget about mattresses and peas. Here are the signs of a true princess—eight virtues that spell out the word *PRINCESS*:

- **Praiseworthiness.** A princess understands that she is worthy of praise simply because she is made in the image of God. The more she understands that she is innately praiseworthy, the more she lives in a praiseworthy manner. She becomes what she already is: praiseworthy.

- **Righteousness.** Though she lives in a fallen world, where everybody walks with a limp, a princess stands straight and walks tall. She lives according to God's normal, not the world's normal. A righteous person isn't simply a person who has to be right all

6

the time; she's a person who is aligned with the right ways that God intended us to live.

- **Initiative.** Because she understands her praiseworthiness, and because her righteousness aligns her with God's best, a princess takes initiative in doing good in the world. A princess makes good things happen.

- **Nurture.** God built into girls and women an instinct for nurture that boys and men simply don't have in the same way. As you nurture your princess, you will equip her to nurture others. And by practicing nurture, she grows toward godly womanhood and will pass that along to her daughters.

- **Character.** A girl of character knows what her deepest desires are and chooses accordingly, ignoring all the short-term and temporary desires and pleasures that might throw her off the trail of her deepest joy. Raising your princess to be a woman of character means helping her get in touch with her truest desires so that she can resist her lesser ones.

- **Empowerment.** A princess possesses great power. Your princess needs to understand that life isn't just something that happens to her. She has the power to choose, the power to make a big difference not only in her own life, but in the lives of others.

- **Servant-heartedness.** A princess finds purpose not in being served, but in serving. It is important for your princess to understand that it is truly a pleasure to serve other people.

- **Stability.** The previous seven virtues can't take root and grow unless you provide your daughter with a stable environment. Stability isn't so much a virtue as the necessary condition for the other seven virtues to grow. As you provide stability for your daughter, she will grow into the kind of person who helps create stability for others.

Each of the following chapters will discuss one of these eight virtues, providing a self-evaluation so you can check how well you are instilling that virtue in your daughter, followed by stories and examples, practical helps and suggestions, and an examination of what the Bible—and especially Proverbs 31—has to say about that virtue.

The Princess in Proverbs 31

Proverbs 31, with its portrait of a godly woman, is one of the best-loved passages in the Bible. You hear it every Mother's Day; you hear it at women's conferences; you hear it at funerals of great matriarchs. You almost always hear it in the context of grown women, not girls.

As I thought through the virtues of a princess, I realized that each of those virtues is exemplified in the Excellent Woman of Proverbs 31. So how do you equip a daughter to become the kind of woman who is described in Proverbs 31? A woman like that, after all, doesn't appear out of nowhere. Somebody taught her to rise before dawn to provide for her household. Somebody gave her the moral compass to reach out her hand to the needy. Somebody taught her the business principles that made it possible for her to consider a field and buy it. Perhaps most important, somebody gave her a sufficiently strong sense of self that made it possible for her to go out and make a huge impact on the world around her.

One of Stephen Covey's "7 Habits of Highly Effective People" is to "begin with the end in mind." This book operates on that principle. The end is the Proverbs 31 Woman; we keep her squarely in view as we look at what parenting techniques help the reader to raise a princess who will someday be somebody's queen.

Chapter 1

Praiseworthiness

Katie is a beautiful girl. At the age of ten she came to Big Oak Ranch out of a hellish environment. She had been beaten and abused on a regular basis for most of her life. When she wasn't being beaten, many times she was being locked in a closet for days at a time. She arrived at the Ranch in clothes that were ragged and dirty and two sizes too small. She possessed zero self-esteem.

But still, she was beautiful. She just didn't believe it. Every chance I got, I told her, "Katie, you're beautiful." She didn't light up when she heard it, the way your daughter might. She didn't even smile. She just looked down at her feet. "Katie," I would persist, "you know it, don't you? Don't you know you're beautiful?" Still, she just kept looking down, shaking her head. No, she didn't know she was beautiful, and it seemed there could be no convincing her. This didn't just happen once or twice. It happened for months.

When a girl lives through what Katie had lived through, her trust muscles are pretty much shredded. When I told her she was beautiful, I was telling her the truth. When I told her she was praiseworthy, I wasn't lying. But she couldn't believe it. Ten years of hearing that you're worthless, useless, a dog to be beaten and worse—that's not something that gets turned around in a few days or a few weeks. It may not get turned around in a few years, or even in a lifetime. When a girl hears the same thing repeated enough times, she begins to believe it. I was going to have to do a lot of repeating to make her believe what I was telling her.

It is a dangerous thing when a girl thinks she's worthless. There's more at stake here than self-esteem (though self-esteem is incredibly important). When a girl thinks she doesn't matter, she thinks her choices don't matter—for good or for bad. She makes the kind of choices that perpetuate cycles that hurt her and the people around her.

Katie spent enough time around the Ranch that she finally came to understand that she was praiseworthy. She paid me one of the greatest compliments of my life when she told one of the new girls, "Mr. John makes you feel like there's nothing wrong with you."

Does your daughter feel like there's nothing wrong with her? I don't mean does your daughter feel that she is sinless or that she can do no wrong. That would cause a whole other set of problems! But she does need to know that she is praiseworthy. She needs to hear from you that she's valuable and lovable just the way God made her. And she needs to hear it often enough that she believes it even when the world tells her that she needs to starve herself to be beautiful or a boy tells her she's going to have to put out if she expects to be loved. A girl who already knows she's praiseworthy is going to laugh at the world as she finishes that cheeseburger. She's going to tell that boy to stick it in his ear. And she's going to be a light and a hope for the girls around her who face the same pressures.

> *She needs to hear from you that she's valuable and lovable just the way God made her.*

The Praiseworthy Woman of Proverbs 31

Proverbs 31 ends with a picture of a queen honored by those whose lives she touched:

Her children rise up and call her blessed;

her husband also, and he praises her:

"Many women have done excellently,

but you surpass them all."

Charm is deceitful, and beauty is vain,

but a woman who fears the LORD is to be praised.

Give her of the fruit of her hands,

and let her works praise her in her gates.

(vv. 28–31)

As always, we're beginning with the end in mind. To know how to raise a princess, we're looking at the queen that she will become.

The queen in this passage is praiseworthy. Her children rise up and call her blessed. Her husband praises her because she has done excellent things. Her reward is her works. She sees the payoff for the good deeds that she has done.

That's where you want your princess to be when she grows into a queen. You want her to be a woman whose good works make her praiseworthy. But how do you get her to that point? What will make your daughter praiseworthy?

The answer may seem simple: When she does works that are worthy of praise, then she will be praiseworthy, right?

Not exactly. Remember, your young daughter is in a different place in life from the woman described in Proverbs 31. As her parent, your job isn't simply to praise her for the good works that she does. Your job is to build in her an understanding that she is praiseworthy simply because she is who God made her. As she grows into that understanding of herself, she will grow into the kind of good works that make it obvious to the rest of the world—and not just her parents—that she is praiseworthy.

We have raised a lot of girls, and here is one thing we have learned: the girls who go out and do great things in the world are the ones who believe that they are worth something, who believe that their actions are actually going to make a difference. A girl whose self-esteem is shattered is a girl who doesn't bother with excellence, whether that's excellence in school work, excellence in serving others, or even moral excellence. She thinks, *What does it matter?* She thinks that an abusive, selfish boyfriend or husband is all she deserves and she settles for what she has been brainwashed to believe about herself, and that is reflected in her life choices. She may engage in people-pleasing to try to get love or attention. But truly sustained excellence of the kind described in Proverbs 31—that only comes from a person who believes that her life has meaning and purpose.

The praiseworthiness of the Proverbs 31 Woman is the kind of praiseworthiness that nobody can deny. Everybody, Christian or non-Christian, wise or foolish, admires a woman who works with willing hands and shows wisdom in business transactions and reaches out to the needy and speaks wisdom. But that obvious praiseworthiness is just the outward expression of an inward praiseworthiness that our girls need help seeing in themselves. Your daughter is made in the image of God. She has unique gifts and talents. She has limitations, and those are God-given too. She needs to know that God wants to work in and through her to do amazing things in her world.

Unconditional Love Builds a Princess

Recently, I was speaking at a national convention. At the airport as I was leaving, a man who had been at the morning's seminar came up with tears in his eyes and said, "When I left home this morning to come to this meeting, my teenage daughter walked up to me and said, 'Daddy, I'm pregnant.' What should I do?"

My response was simple: "Your first mistake was getting on the airplane to come here. You should have stayed at home with your little girl."

Anybody can make a girl feel praiseworthy when they are doing good. Can you give them that same feeling when a mistake has been made, or they have not lived up to a standard, *or* embarrassed the family name?

So many people have had that conversation throughout history and it has revealed numerous responses from parents. Statements like, "How could you do this to me and your mom?" or "I knew you were gonna do this. You're on your own!"

Let me share with you the rest of what I told this man in the airport. "Go home, take your daughter in your arms, and hold her for a couple of minutes. Don't talk or say anything, just hold her, then look her in the eyes and say something like, 'This wasn't what we had planned and I know you are really hurting right now and we are too. I want you to listen to me, you're my baby girl, my princess, and I love you no matter what!"

With every ounce of love you possess, tell your baby girl, "I'm here and we will get through this together."

We had a young girl who grew up at the Ranch. After she left us to go out on her own, she made a mistake like this and because our staff did such a great job letting her know she still was loved unconditionally, she is now married and is a great wife to her husband and a great mom to her little girl. She *is* praiseworthy!

> *With every ounce of love you possess tell your baby girl, "I'm here and we will get through this together."*

The core of building praiseworthiness in your princess is her knowing beyond a shadow of a doubt that you have unconditional love for her even when she behaves poorly. You are in her corner and will support her through ups and downs, highs and lows.

Praiseworthiness You Can't Hide

I realize that I am ridiculously biased, but my daughter Reagan is a very beautiful young woman. You don't have to take my word for it. After college, she had a modeling career here and in Europe. So obviously I'm not the only one who thinks she's beautiful.

One day when she was modeling with Elite Modeling Agency in Milan, Italy, Reagan showed up at work and the stylist gave her a cellophane dress to put on. She took one look at the dress and said, "I don't wear see-through dresses."

The stylist was shocked. "What do you mean you don't wear see-through dresses?" he sputtered. "If you expect to have a modeling career, you'll wear what we tell you to wear." Reagan handed the dress back to him and left.

As it turns out, the stylist was wrong. Walking out that day wasn't the end of her modeling career; she actually got a much better modeling job the very next day. But the point is that Reagan was willing to accept the possibility that walking away from that opportunity might end her career. She would rather be herself and be unemployed than compromise herself for the sake of a modeling career.

It was a praiseworthy deed, and it made me about as proud of my daughter as I have ever been. Where did that kind of self-worth come from? A lot of it came from the fact that Reagan already knew that she was praiseworthy. She didn't need the approval of that stylist or the photographer or the fashion industry or the people who read fashion magazines in order to feel that she was worth something.

Every day of her life, Reagan had heard that she was a princess, and she believed it long before she ever entered into any modeling contract. To lose a modeling career would have been no great blow to her sense of self. That confidence is a big part of what makes Reagan so beautiful. See the irony? The quality that equipped her to be a model in the first place was the same quality that made her hold very lightly to her modeling career.

A woman with that kind of confidence is pretty dangerous, in the best sense. A woman who knows she's praiseworthy has no fear. She is free to say "stick it in your ear" to anybody who wants her to compromise her integrity—to anyone who offers her false value.

Practical Helps and Suggestions

So how do you instill praiseworthiness in your daughter? Remember, our goal here is to help our daughters see that they are *already* praiseworthy so that they will act accordingly. You're not waiting around for her to do praise-worthy things so you can praise her for them. You're being proactive.

Performance-oriented parenting says, "Perform for me, and I will give you praise." Princess-oriented parenting works the other way around. It's very much like our relationship with God. We don't obey so that God will love us. We obey out of gratitude as we begin to grasp how much God already loves us.

Here are some practical tips for instilling praiseworthiness in your daughter.

Pay Attention

Get in the habit of noticing the good things that your daughter is doing, whether that is helping someone else or working really hard at something that doesn't come easy for her. And then verbalize what you have noticed; put it in words for your daughter. All of us need love and sincere praise. Every now and then, put it in writing. It will take you two to three minutes to get a pen and paper and knock out a quick note telling your daughter something about her that makes you proud. She will treasure it for as long as she lives.

Also, get in the habit of taking pictures. When your daughter is dressed up and looking beautiful, take a picture to remember the night. When she has mud in her pigtails, take a picture of that too. Picture-taking communicates to your daughter that you value her so much that you want to be able to remember her just the way she is at that moment in time.

Paying attention may cost you something, by the way. If you have a time-consuming hobby that takes you away from home a lot, especially on Saturday, when your daughter has her soccer game or ballet recital, you might need a different hobby, at least until your daughter grows up. She may not remember the events, games, recitals, etc., that you came to, but she will never forget the ones you missed. Children *always* know what's more important to you than they are.

Give Your Daughter Opportunities to Excel

Figure out what your daughter is good at, or what she's passionate about, and help her to pursue those interests. Sign her up for a softball league (better yet, coach her team), sign her up for dance lessons, talk to her about the books she's reading in school. If she has a heart for serving others, help her figure out how to do that. I know a family that has put on a 5K fund-raiser for an orphanage in Africa every year for the last ten years because their daughter, a runner, expressed an interest in African orphans.

Everybody is good at something. Good parenting is finding out what your child is good at and helping them develop those God-given talents. So many times I see girls come to Big Oak Ranch who have never had an opportunity to excel in anything—not because they lacked talents or interests, but because nobody in their life was willing to go to the effort to help pursue them.

> Everybody is good at something. Good parenting is finding out what your child is good at and helping them develop those God-given talents.

You've seen the stage moms and the sports-driven dads who push their kids so hard at pageants or athletics that their kids never want to see a tiara or a soccer ball again. I'm not encouraging you to be that kind of parent. It doesn't do anybody any good when you live your unfulfilled dreams vicariously through your kids. I'm talking about giving your kids the chance to push themselves and learn that they can accomplish more than they thought they could.

Tell the Truth

False praise won't help your daughter's self-esteem. When she discovers that she's not actually the greatest chess player in the world—after you've let her win every time you've ever played and praised her to the heavens—she's going to be back to square one in the self-esteem department, and she's going to be less likely to believe you when you give her legitimate praise. On the other hand, if you praise her because she's better at chess today than she was last month, you're building her up in truth.

We live in a world where every kid on the team gets a trophy, even though nobody was keeping score during the game. It's supposed to be good for the kids' self-esteem. It isn't. What's good for kids' self-esteem is when adults they care about tell them the truth in a constructive way. There is plenty about your daughter that you can truthfully praise if you're paying attention. You don't need to create fictional praise. They will resent you and will not value the "participation" trophy. On the other hand, an honest, sincere compliment is priceless in building your little girl's self-esteem.

Focus on the Process Rather than the Result

As you build up your daughter, pay more attention to the process by which she strives for success than to the result. When your daughter has to struggle for a B-, but she actually goes through the struggle, that's more praiseworthy than the A she gets without really having to try.

A few years ago, some psychologists did a study in which they gave a bunch of kids a simple problem that they could all easily solve. For half the kids, they said, "Good job. You must really be smart." For the other half of the kids, they said, "Good job. You must have really tried hard." They repeated this with several other relatively easy problems, congratulating half the kids on their smarts, and congratulating the other half of the kids on their work ethic. But then they gave the kids a problem that wasn't easy. The kids who had been praised for their intelligence mostly failed to solve the problem. They looked at it, decided it was beyond their intelligence, and quit. But the other kids—the ones who had been praised for their ability to work hard—rolled up their sleeves, got to work, and succeeded at a much higher rate than the "smart" kids.

If your daughter is smart, beautiful, or a natural athlete, praise her for it and teach her to be thankful for her God-given gifts. But look especially for opportunities to praise her for character issues like perseverance, kindness, and honor—things that she actually has some control over. These are the qualities that are really going to make her a world-changer.

Help Your Daughter See the Bigger Picture

Hopefully, you are able to see a much bigger picture than your daughter can. Help her see how her gifts, talents, and passions fit into the greater work of honoring the Lord with her life. When you see her putting a Band-Aid on her doll, you could say, "Aww, how cute!" Or you could say, "I love to see you taking such good care of your doll. You might make a great doctor when you grow up and help a lot of people who are sick."

Don't just praise your daughter's good qualities; help her see how God could use them for His good purposes. Help her realize all God meant for her to be. He gave her those qualities to accomplish something greater than she realizes. Just as you can see a bigger picture than your daughter can, God can see a much bigger picture than either of you.

Control Your Anger

"Whoever is slow to anger is better than the mighty, and he who rules his spirit than he who takes a city" (Prov. 16:32). Kids can be exasperating, but it is vital that you control your anger. To a young girl, an adult's anger can be overwhelming—especially a man's anger. If she feels you're angry with her, it can neutralize quite a lot of praise. I'm not just talking about explosive, violent anger. What seems to you like a minor expression of anger or irritation might seem to her like a major outburst. You think you're tossing a pebble, but she feels like you're heaving a boulder.

Unless you're a very unusual parent, there will be times when you slip up and show anger toward your children. In that case, your willingness to repent toward your children and ask for their forgiveness will prove to be an extremely valuable moment of healing, as well as an important lesson for your daughter.

Be Respectful toward Her Mother

If you are a father, remember that loving your children's mother is one of the best things that you can do for your children. You are modeling the way women should be treated. One day, when your daughter chooses a husband, she is probably going to choose a man who treats her the way her mother has been treated by her father.

By the way, this principle applies even if you are divorced. Your daughter should never hear you bad-mouthing her mother, even if the two of you aren't married. Careless words can do irreparable damage and create instability in your little girl's heart.

Help Your Daughter Survive Her Mistakes

Your daughter is going to mess up. She may even mess up in a big way. You need to be ready to handle that. One of the principal truths of the Christian faith is that our past does not determine our future. When your daughter makes a mis-take, she needs to know that even if she has to live through painful con-sequences, that mistake doesn't cancel out the good things in her life. She is still your princess; she is still praiseworthy; and she isn't disqualified from doing important work for God, who loves to bring good things out of bad messes. As a parent, it is important that you not compound her mistake with mistakes of your own in handling her situation.

> *When your daughter makes a mistake, she needs to know that even if she has to live through painful consequences, that mistake doesn't cancel out the good things in her life.*

Conclusion

We all want our daughters to be praiseworthy. We want them to be the kind of people whose character and good deeds attract the notice of everybody who knows them. But if our daughters are going to be that kind of people, they need some help from us, their parents.

Negative focus does not build praiseworthiness. Your daughter's worth, just like yours, comes from what God sees when he looks at her. But on a much smaller scale, her praiseworthiness begins with you, her parent, seeing things in her that she can't yet see in herself. She needs to know what you see in her. Anyone can point out mistakes. Successful parenting is recognizing and building on the positives.

Chapter 2

Righteousness

 Imagine a world where everybody walks hunched over and with a limp. People would come to believe that hunching and limping is normal, even the best way to walk. They would convince themselves that all those pains they feel from misalignment—the back trouble, the displaced hips, the headaches—are just normal, unavoidable facts of life.

Now imagine what would happen in such a world if a few people stood up tall and walked straight. Everybody else would think they were freaks. They would point and laugh. Some would take these straight-walkers aside and tell them that they were making a spectacle of themselves. Some would give them advice: "Put these rocks in one of your shoes, and you'll be limping in no time." Some would think the straight-walkers were putting on airs. A few would try to trip the straight-walkers, to prove that their way of walking isn't better after all.

It would be hard to be a straight-walker in a world where everybody limps. These precious few might have doubts: Is it worth going through the ridicule and the ill will? Wouldn't it be easier just to limp like everybody else? Except for this: the straight-walkers notice that their backs don't hurt anymore. Their hips feel strong, their heads feel clear. They didn't know how much pain their limps had caused until they tried walking upright. They feel stronger. They run faster. They don't tire so easily. They just feel better overall because they are walking as they were designed to do.

Actually, we do live in a world where everyone limps. This world is bent by sin, made lame by it. And so the world thinks that what is bent is actually straight, or at least normal. Anybody who chooses not to conform to the brokenness is looked on as a freak.

The second characteristic that I consider of a princess is righteousness. Righteousness just means standing up tall and walking straight in a world where hunching over and limping through life has come to be viewed as normal. Righteousness isn't about following rules or being so right that you prove everybody else is wrong. Righteousness doesn't have anything to do with passing judgment on anybody else. It is never arrogant or *self*-righteous. It's about living the way you were meant to live, regardless of what the world around you is doing—a way that feels "right."

That's what we all want for our daughters, isn't it? We want them to live lives that are right—not right as in "I'm right and you're wrong," but right as in "I know this is right." Right as in the way she lives matches up with the way God created her, and things are in alignment.

The girls who come to Big Oak Ranch come from settings where things are more bent than usual. When abuse and neglect are all you've ever known, of course you're going to think it's normal to be abused and neglected. Why wouldn't you assume

> *Right as in the way she lives matches up with the way God created her, and things are in alignment.*

that's the way things are always going to be? One of our first goals for every girl who comes to the Ranch is to give her a chance to see what God's normal can feel like, so she can see that things she looked at as normal aren't normal at all.

For some girls, it feels like standing up straight for the first time. It's as if they say, "Oh! I knew there was something wrong with the life I was stuck in! This is more like it!" That's the beginning of righteousness—the moral equivalent of getting your spine adjusted so that things are in alignment and everything starts working better and you just feel better.

For most girls, it's not an immediate thing. They see a new way of living, but they're so used to their old way of living that it takes some time to embrace God's normal. Sadly, some girls never do come around.

Years ago we got a girl who, as far back as she could remember, had been molested by her father. I sat her down the first day she came to the ranch and I told her, "That's never going to happen to you again. It wasn't right what your father did to you, but now you're safe."

She looked me straight in the face and said, "You're wrong."

"No, baby," I said. "I'm not wrong. I'm telling you, that kind of thing isn't going to happen here."

She said, "That's not what I meant."

I was confused.

"I meant you were wrong when you said the things my daddy did wasn't right. That's just how little girls show their daddies that they love them. My daddy told me so himself."

I had the same talk with that girl many times. And every time she said, "You're wrong. That's how girls show their daddies that they love them." Within a year, this girl decided she didn't want to live at the Ranch and that what we were teaching her wasn't what she believed to be true. She never accepted the fact that the life she came from wasn't normal.

To raise a righteous girl is to raise a girl who can see the difference between God's normal and what passes for "normal" in the world around her. It is our job as parents to help them see that God's normal leads to a genuine joy that goes far beyond the short-term pleasures of fitting in with a world that walks with a limp.

The Righteousness of the Proverbs 31 Woman

In Proverbs 31, Solomon uses an unusual, even surprising image to describe an Excellent Woman. "She is like the merchant ships," he says in verse 14 (NKJV). And then, in verse 18, he writes, "She perceives that her merchandise is good" (NKJV). I think that image gives us an interesting way to think about righteousness.

People mean a lot of different things when they use the word *righteous*. Obviously, one key goal of righteousness is to sin less. But one thing that Proverbs 31 clearly expresses is that merely avoiding sin is a low goal. The Excellent Woman of Proverbs 31 isn't just avoiding sin, but actively doing well in the world. She's going out like a merchant ship, bringing "goods" to the world and bringing "goods" back home to her family.

There are cultures whose whole concept of preserving a woman's righteousness is to take away opportunities to commit sin. Women are covered up, locked up, prevented from driving or going to school or being in public without a husband or male relative by her side. Though in our overly permissive culture that may sometimes seem like an attractive option, my point is that you can't create righteousness by taking away opportunities to sin.

We want to shelter our daughters from the dangers of a culture that seems determined to turn girls into materialistic bimbos who spend all their time on their cell phones communicating with people they barely know. And make no mistake: sheltering our daughters is part of the plan for raising them into truly righteous women. But sheltering is not and cannot be the whole plan for instilling righteousness in our daughters. Sin, after all, doesn't only come as the result of outward temptations. Even in our sweet little daughters, sin comes from the heart. Outward temptations provide convenient opportunities for the sin to come out; but the real issue is our daughters' hearts. That's where the real work of becoming a princess has to happen.

The Excellent Woman of Proverbs 31 goes out like the merchant ships. She is in the middle of the back-and-forth of her culture. Why isn't her husband concerned about this? Because he knows that she is a righteous woman. She stands tall and walks straight no matter what the people around her are doing. And when she goes out into the world, it's the world who had better watch out. She brings a different vision that puts the world's vision to shame. "She opens her mouth with wisdom," verse 26 says, "And on her tongue is the law of kindness" (NKJV). Remember, this is a woman who mixes it up in the cutthroat world of business. She buys and sells fabric. She buys real estate. And yet on her tongue is the law of kindness. She knows what is good and right; she's going to live by God's normal, not by the world's normal.

I think it is unique that Solomon chose a commercial image to describe his Excellent Woman. In Solomon's world, what could be more commercial than a merchant ship, leaving the security of home and going out to do business with all different kinds of people from all different backgrounds? It's intriguing because we don't normally think of women in those terms. But it's also intriguing because we live in such a highly commercialized culture ourselves. You and I faced plenty of temptations when we were young. But they weren't so closely tied to constant, in-your-face marketing pushed by clever people with lots and lots of money. Your daughter, from the first time she became aware of what was going on around her, was connected to the commercialism of American culture—and the temptations that go along with it. Maybe the typical ancient-biblical-times woman wasn't especially involved with the commercial aspects of her culture. But your daughter is. It's as if Solomon had twenty-first-century women in mind when he compared his Excellent Woman to a merchant ship.

It may seem like we've gotten away from righteousness with all this business about merchant ships and commercialism. Verse 18 should bring it back around: "She perceives that her merchandise is good" (NKJV). You could hardly hope for a better summary of what it is like to be a righteous woman in the middle of an unrighteous culture. Somewhere along the line, somebody taught that woman how to "do business" with the world and still remain untainted. She ignored the hucksters and pushed past the people selling inferior merchandise and avoided the crooks, and she managed to lay hold of those things that are truly valuable. She lives in confidence, knowing that her merchandise is good—not only the merchandise she buys or acquires, but also the merchandise that she offers to the world.

> *When you raise a princess, you aren't preparing her for a life of sheltered innocence. You're preparing her to stand tall and walk straight in a world where most people limp.*

When you raise a princess, you aren't preparing her for a life of sheltered innocence. You're preparing her to stand tall and walk straight in a world where most people limp. Of course you have to provide shelter and cover when she's young. But as always, we're beginning with the end in mind. And the end is a righteous woman who influences the world instead of letting the world influence her. And the key principle is to help her see that God's idea of normal is a better, more satisfying way to live than the world's idea of normal.

Standing Up-Right

All of the kids who live at Big Oak Ranch go to Westbrook Christian School, but it's not just Ranch kids at the school. There are hundreds of kids from all over the community who also attend the school. You can imagine how hard it is for most of the new Ranch kids to find their way into the mainstream. Private Christian school hasn't been their scene; it seems like another world for many of these kids. For the most part, though, they manage to fit in eventually.

I spend a lot of time at Westbrook, and there's a scene I've seen played out over and over again. On the one hand there are the "regular" girls—the girls who don't live at the Ranch. They're mainstream, they know their place, and they seem (on the outside at least) to "have it together." On the other hand, there's a new Ranch girl. She's awkward and scared. She's not sure where to go or what to do. She feels like she's never going to have it together like those "regular" girls do. And then, smack in the middle, is one of the Ranch girls who have been with us for a while. A year or two ago she was right where that new girl is now. Slowly but surely, she worked her way up the pecking order so that she finally fit in with the "regular" girls. And now she has a choice: she can take her hard-earned place among those girls, who are nice enough but don't have any way of knowing what that new girl is going through, or she can risk her status by going over to the new girl and making sure she feels welcome. It's the "old" Ranch girl who I always watch. I always wonder whether she's going to choose righteousness. She's the one who has the most at stake.

It's not that the mainstream girls are bad. They're going with the flow (there's a reason they call it the "mainstream," after all). Most of the time righteousness requires going against the flow. It's walking straight when everyone else walks with a limp.

When my daughter Reagan was in the seventh grade, she came home from school one day and said, "I hit somebody today." I was shocked. Reagan was not exactly a brawler. "You're in seventh grade," I said. "You're too old to be hitting people. Who did you hit?" "A twelfth-grade boy. He wouldn't stop picking on one of the Ranch girls. So I hit him."

Ah . . . that was another thing altogether. That wasn't brawling. That was righteous anger. And while I'm willing to admit that hitting people may not be the best way to express righteous anger, I also have to admit that I was pretty proud of my "little" girl, who chose to stand up for somebody who was in no position to stand up for herself. Reagan could have gone with the flow, but instead she stood up and fought back. It's "normal" for the strong to pick on the weak. In fighting back against that "normality," Reagan was asserting a different kind of normal. "This is God's normal," she was saying. "There's a better normality than the one the world asks us to accept."

I'm especially sensitive to this kind of righteousness because I live with the shame of a time when I went with the mainstream instead of choosing righteousness. There was a girl named Mary at my middle school. She was tall and gangly and was considered not very pretty. She wore the same dress every day. I guess that meant she almost never had a chance to wash it, because it was always filthy. Mary smelled terrible. So people made fun of her constantly.

Whenever we did any kind of dancing at school, the teachers paired us up by height. Mary was the tallest girl. I was the tallest boy. That meant we were partners every time we danced. It also meant that I was in a unique position to show Mary kindness and compassion. I could have been a rare bright spot in her dark life. But I chose a different path. I moaned and complained and held my nose. When the teacher made us assume dancing position, I stood as far away from her as my long arms allowed and barely touched her. If it was true I was in a good position to encourage Mary and build her up, it was also true that I was in a good position to tear her down. And that's exactly what I did.

I don't know what became of Mary. She dropped out of school as soon as she was able to, and none of us ever heard from her again. Who can blame her? I don't believe I could have survived the kind of rejection she experienced at school every day. I can't help but believe that just a little bit of kindness would have made a huge difference for Mary. But she didn't get any from me. I was too wrapped up in my own efforts to fit in and go with the flow.

Part of my problem was the fact that I felt a little bit like Mary myself. I was kind of an ugly kid. My ugliness was so well-known, in fact, that when we played away games in junior and senior high, the fans of the opposing team would make up chants about my ugliness—many of them too awful to repeat here.

I'm not making excuses for the way I treated Mary. I'm saying that because I felt that I was on the losing end of schoolyard politics, it never occurred to me that there was a better way. Looking back I can see that I needed to be sure there was at least one person below me in the pecking order.

The righteous thing would have been to forget about the pecking order altogether.

Of course righteousness is about more than reaching out to the kids who are not in the "in crowd." I use these examples because they are a good gauge for the big picture. If your daughter can go against the flow at school and opt out of the whole pecking order drama, she can go against the flow in a lot of other things. She can dress modestly when most everybody else is leaving little to the imagination. She can turn down the beer and the pot at the party. She can kick that boy to the curb when he says that she's a prude for not letting him use her.

Most parents think the "mean girl" dramas of middle school are minor compared to the "big" sins of sex and drugs. I would suggest that if you can help set your daughter free from the dramas that play out in the lunchroom and the hallways, you have gone a long way toward setting her free from the dramas that play out at parties and in the backseats of cars. Your daughter needs to know that there is a better "normal" than the one she sees at school and on television. As she embraces that righteous normality she knows and feels it is right no matter what anyone says.

Practical Helps and Suggestions

So how do you encourage righteousness in your daughter? Give her a vision that goes beyond the limited vision that she gets from school and from ever-present media. She needs to see that God's way is better than the world's way. That's going to require that you be very intentional. The world, after all, has advertising and marketing and the media on its side. And peer pressure. And every social insecurity that every girl feels. All these things work against God's normal. It is hard for a young girl to stand tall and walk straight in a world of limpers. Your daughter needs a lot of help and support from you. Here are some things to do to help your daughter walk upright and live in God's normal.

> *It is hard for a young girl to stand tall and walk straight in a world of limpers. Your daughter needs a lot of help and support from you.*

Teach your daughter that righteousness means freedom, not rule-keeping.

If your daughter believes that righteousness means conformity to certain rules, she isn't going to live a righteousness that lasts. She might keep your rules while she's at home, but eventually she's going to throw those rules out the window. Your daughter needs to understand that to be righteous is to be free from the belief that she has to conform to the world around her.

Take modesty as an example. If your approach to modesty is simply to set rules about where hemlines and necklines have to be, you aren't getting to the heart of the matter. Your daughter might conform. Or maybe she'll leave the house feeling like she is dressed like a prude and then change into a mini-skirt and halter-top at the first gas station bathroom she comes to. Either way, you've created a situation in which your daughter's goal is to keep you happy and off her case. It has nothing to do with her heart.

On the other hand, you could sit down with your daughter and say, "Darling, the world wants to tell you that you have to show a certain amount of leg and a certain amount of cleavage if you want to be loved. That's just a big lie. You don't have to be a slave to all that. You're free. You don't have to be a conformist." And sure, give her some guidelines for how to dress. But put those guidelines in the context of freedom. We are free from the demands of the world. The human heart responds to the call to freedom; if your daughter understands that righteousness is freedom, the battle is more than half won.

Understand that it is hard for your daughter to be righteous.

To go against the world's normal is going to cause your daughter some pain. The desire to fit in is one of the strongest desires that a young girl feels. Conformity is a hard thing to let go of. Your daughter needs to know that her reluctance to go against the flow is normal and understandable. It's not proof that she is a bad person or that she doesn't have what it takes to be righteous. She doesn't need to beat herself up, nor does she need simply to give in to the temptation to live the way the world says is right.

The other day I was in the lobby at the Girls' Ranch and one of our girls was leaving to go to a special place to help her get through and over her past abuse. We have secured her a spot in a program that has remarkable success with children like her who have been abused beyond comprehension. She's beyond our ability to help, so we are getting her more in-depth treatment—we are *not* giving up on her. We are getting more professional help in order to help her "win" over the issues of her past that are continuing to make her walk with a limp. She was anxious and scared to be leaving the Ranch to go to this place.

I told her, "After having both of my knees replaced over the last nine months, I had to hurt really bad and go through intense pain and therapy, but now I feel better than I have felt in twenty years. If I had it to do over again, I would have had the surgeries years ago, but my fear kept me from it. I now have little to no pain in my knees. I had no idea how much pain I was in until I wasn't feeling it anymore."

Our daughters have to know that sometimes they have to leave their sense of normal, their "comfort zone," and go through pain and discomfort in order to come out on the other side standing straight and walking tall, and living God's normal!

Explain to your daughter that, even though times are now different, you can relate to the pain and discomfort and loneliness caused by living according to a normality that is different from the normality around you. But also reassure her that as she learns to stand up straight, she will be freed from pains that she didn't even know she was feeling.

Help your daughter be a wise consumer of media.

Let's face it: a life of steady faithfulness and service seems a little un-glamorous compared to the celebrity life that is portrayed on television, on the Internet, and in magazines. Our kids' days are so media-saturated that the over-the-top selfishness and materialism portrayed in the media can seem more normal than real life. To a child, the values of reality TV, pop music, and air-brushed glamour can seem like something actually to aspire to.

It is extremely important that you talk to your daughter about the media she consumes. When you watch TV with her, ask questions:

1. What would the world be like if everybody lived like that?
2. What do you think that person had to give up to be that famous? What would you be willing to give up in order to be famous?
3. Are the vices and temptations seen on television worth the compromise they require?
4. Why do you think Hollywood is full of stories of child celebrities and actors "losing it"?

So many times, we parents just ignore the inappropriate things that our kids see on television or on the covers of magazines in the grocery checkout. It's uncomfortable. But when we don't speak, our kids assume all that must be normal. Next time you're buying groceries, speak to your daughter about the women on the magazine cover. She needs to know that those women are probably air-brushed, and that even if they're not, they aren't the norm.

My point is that your daughter needs to be reassured that standing tall is the correct way to live—period. The glamour portrayed in the media isn't as great as it looks. True fulfillment is attainable and is closer at hand than she may think.

Talk to your daughter about your experiences at her age.

Even though times are *so* different now, your daughter needs to know that you know what it is like to be in her shoes. Tell her about the time you failed to stick up for a kid who was being bullied. Tell her what you did to make it right. Or tell her about the regret you felt for not making it right. Your daughter doesn't need to see you as perfect. She needs to see that you have struggled, where you won and where you lost.

Obviously, be discerning here. I'm not suggesting that you tell your daughter about every sin you ever committed as a teenager. And I'm certainly not telling you to detail your sins in any way that would make your daughter feel justified in following in those particular footsteps. But there is a lot to be gained from letting your daughter know that you understand where she's coming from.

> *Your daughter doesn't need to see you as perfect. She needs to see that you have struggled, where you won and where you lost.*

Make sure your daughter sees you living by God's normal.

Your daughter listens with her eyes. If she sees you living according to the standards of the world, living only for yourself, not respecting others, not standing up for the weak, then no amount of talking on your part is going to convince her that righteousness is a better way to live. Living righteously yourself is the best way to teach your daughter God's normal.

Conclusion

When I was in third grade, I had a teacher named Mrs. Sims. She was a righteous woman. Third grade was a very hard time in my life. My little sister had died a few years earlier. I was traumatized by that experience, and my parents were in such deep grief that they simply didn't have the resources to help me through it.

I had a puppy that meant more to me than almost anything in the world. After watching calf-roping on television, I got the idea to tie up my puppy. I accidentally tied it up too tight and hurt it. My father came along about that time and, concerned for the puppy's safety, threatened to take it away from me. In my frustration and shame, I started clawing at my face. I shredded myself from my cheeks to my collarbones before my father managed to stop me.

The next day at school, I was embarrassed for anybody to see my face. Mrs. Sims took one look at me and asked me what had happened. I answered, "My daddy is gonna give my dog away!" I just started crying. Mrs. Sims immediately called recess and sent everybody but me out of the room. She pulled me onto her lap and just hugged me. I still remember the smell of her perfume and the feel of one hand on my rib cage, the other on my knee. She didn't say anything. She just let me cry it out. I had felt so lonely when I got to school that morning, but Mrs. Sims made me feel that everything was going to be okay.

A few years ago, I ran into Mrs. Sims again. She and her husband came to a talk I gave, and afterwards she came up and asked if I knew who she was. I was so glad to see her. I said, "Mrs. Sims, there's something I want to thank you for. Do you remember the time you sat me on your lap and just let me cry?"

Mrs. Sims gave me that same sweet smile I had seen so often when I was a scared little eight-year-old. "No, John," she said. "I'm afraid I don't remember that at all."

I was shocked. How could she not remember that? It was one of the most memorable moments of my life! Her kindness gave me hope and got me through a time when I didn't have any idea how I was going to get through.

Her husband was standing behind her, and he was just bawling. "This kind of thing happens all the time," he said.

"Somebody comes up to her and asks if she remembers some good deed that changed their life. And most of the time she doesn't remember it at all." He patted his wife on the back. "It's just the way she has always lived her life. That kind of goodness just pours out of her. There are just too many good deeds to remember."

That's true righteousness. That's what we want for our girls. In the way she lived her life, Mrs. Sims showed what God's idea of normal looked like. She reached a point where she wasn't necessarily consciously choosing to be righteous; it was just a lifestyle. But whether she was thinking about those good deeds or not, I can guarantee you that she was causing other people to think.

Sometimes when we hear the word *righteous*, we think of the kind of people who make others feel uncomfortable or judged. Mrs. Sims showed that a truly righteous person makes other people feel better without even having to try.

Chapter 3

Initiative

 Have you ever taken a good look at a tulip bulb? There's not a whole lot to see. It's just a brown little ball, a little smaller and a little squattier than a hen's egg. If you didn't know what it was, you would never know that it was destined to become one of the most beautiful flowers you've ever seen.

Your daughter is a little like a tulip bulb. Just looking at her, it may be hard to predict what the future holds for this just-born, wrinkly ball of humanity. But it's her destiny to grow into something glorious. Your job as her parent is to nurture her and help her get there.

Remember the scene when the prophet Samuel showed up at the house of Jesse looking for a new king? Jesse proudly showed the prophet his sons—big, strapping boys who looked like they would make kings. Samuel gave each boy a once-over. They were impressive. But God told Samuel that they weren't what he was looking for.

Samuel turned to Jesse and asked, "Are all your sons here?" Only then did Jesse remember the youngest, a shepherd boy named David. They rounded the boy up, and Samuel knew he had found the person he was looking for. David would grow into the greatest earthly king that Israel ever had.

Samuel had a vision for David that even David's own father didn't have. Jesse saw a little kid who made a pretty good shepherd boy. But a king? Jesse suffered from a lack of imagination. He was too busy looking at what was right in front of him to see how bright his son's future could be.

We probably shouldn't be too hard on Jesse. First of all, it seems a little delusional to believe that your own son is going to be king someday. And second, we can all be guilty of the same thing. We all sell our daughters short sometimes. We look at what is in front of us right now and forget that this little girl is destined to be a great woman of God someday.

It takes vision and imagination to help our daughters step into their calling. We treasure them just the way they are, and that is good and right, but it is also our job as parents to help them grow beyond where they are right now. It is our job to help give them the initiative to grow into their specific talents, gifts, and passions. Do you know what your daughter's gifts and passions are? Are you helping her to develop them?

Of the hundreds of kids to come through Big Oak Ranch, most were the first in their families to graduate from high school or much less go on to college. They came from families where that kind of dream was usually squashed. Their parents didn't go to college, they didn't value college; in many cases, those parents didn't want their kids to be overly ambitious and get the idea that they were better than their parents. It

> *It is our job to help give them the initiative to grow into their specific talents, gifts, and passions.*

was the old, "If it was good enough for me, why isn't it good enough for you?" routine.

You may have heard the "crab in the bucket" story. Put several crabs in a bucket or pail. When they try to climb out, they crawl up on each other's back. Just when one gets to the very edge and freedom is so close, he gets pulled back down into the bucket with the rest of the crabs. This happens repeatedly. Nearly every child who goes home for a weekend visit returns to the Ranch with the same experience. Their families, most of the time, say, "Oh, you think you are better than us now." This kind of parenting robs a girl of her initiative. It drags her down to her parents' level, and she very likely ends up dropping out of school, maybe getting a GED, getting a job, and having babies at an early age.

If you're reading this book, you're probably not robbing your daughter of her initiative in that particular way. But there are other, more "respectable" ways that we rob our kids' initiative:

1. **Simply not paying attention.** Sometimes parents are too absorbed in their own pursuits to help their daughters grow into the people God made them to be.

2. **Living out our own dreams through our daughters.** Your daughter isn't your opportunity to relive your glory days or to do a "do-over" of the things you wish you had done when you were her age. She has her own aspirations. Help her live out hers rather than using her to live out yours.

3. **Overdoing it.** Your daughter loves soccer? Great. Get her on a team. If she's interested and you can afford it, take her to clinics, get her a personal coach. But be careful not to push her so hard with travel teams and clinics and off-season training that she burns out before she even gets to high school. I see it all the time: a kid has some interest or some ability in a particular area (especially an area that could result in a college scholarship), and the parents are

so "supportive" that the poor kid will do anything just to get some relief.

This chapter, like chapter 1 on praiseworthiness, is about supporting your daughter and giving her confidence. In chapter 1, that confidence was based on the fact that she is loved and made in the image of God. There's a slight but significant difference in the confidence we're building in this chapter on initiative. Here we're talking about helping your daughter develop specific skills that are related to her interests and passions. "Praiseworthiness" is more general, whereas the initiative we're talking about in this chapter is related to your daughter living out her particular calling.

The Initiative of the Proverbs 31 Woman

Look at how many different ways the Excellent Woman of Proverbs 31 shows initiative:

- She seeks out wool and flax.
- She works with willing hands.
- She goes out into the world like a merchant ship.
- She's up before daylight.
- She buys real estate.
- She makes a profit and builds a vineyard.
- She reaches out to the needy.
- She makes linen garments and sells them.

This woman is kicking butt and taking names. How does she even find time to do all of this stuff?

I notice two things that this Excellent Woman obviously had: a particular attitude and particular skills. In chapter 1 we discussed the way that affirming a girl's praiseworthiness puts her in a frame of mind for success. The parents of the Proverbs 31 Woman convinced her that she was worth something, and that her work was therefore worth something. That kind of attitude motivates a person to go out and "work as unto the Lord."

But the Excellent Woman of Proverbs 31 obviously had something that went beyond a good attitude. She had real skills. Somebody, presumably her parents, taught her how to negotiate business deals, appraise property, run a vineyard, weave cloth, and sell her wares, along with all the skills that go with those activities. The things this woman does aren't just things you pick up casually. Somebody was investing in her.

The incredible initiative and drive of this woman is not what you would normally expect from most people in our day and time. But it's *really* not what you would expect from a woman in ancient biblical times. When Solomon wrote the Proverbs, women were not treated with a lot of respect. There was a Jewish prayer (actually written a few centuries after Solomon's time) that said, "Blessed are you, Lord our God, Ruler of the Universe, who has not made me a woman."[1]

That gives you some idea of how much respect men gave women in that culture. Yet this woman's parents apparently thought highly enough of their little girl to equip her with some serious skills. It didn't matter what society tried to dictate. Did her father take her along to watch him make business deals? Did he show her how to grow a vineyard? Surely her mother taught her how to weave cloth. I don't want to speculate too much on something that the Bible isn't specific about, but I do want to suggest this: The people who raised the Proverbs 31 Woman must have been pretty countercultural. They went against the grain of their culture and said, "You may not value this little girl or the woman she is going to become, but we do." They instilled incredible initiatives even by the standards of our present-day culture, where women have a lot more opportunities to show initiative and perform the work that men do.

Here's the main thing I want you to see about raising a daughter with initiative: you have to be countercultural. If you go with the cultural flow in your parenting, you normally aren't going to end up with a daughter who shows the initiative to go out and take care of her family and serve the needy and have an impact on the world around her. If the culture of Solomon's place and time didn't value women, you'd better believe our culture values them even less. Oh, I know that women in twenty-first-century America are allowed to vote and own property and have pretty much any job a man can have. That's all well and good. But women in our culture are also reduced to sex objects in ways that were unimaginable in Solomon's time. Our girls starve themselves in the belief that they have to be skinnier to be lovable. They cut themselves just to ease their inner pain. I asked one of our new girls, "Why cut?" She replied, "This pain feels better than the pain inside me. This brings me relief."

We live in a culture in which it is getting easier and easier to lose your moorings and just to drift, with no purpose, no initiative. To go with the flow in today's culture is to end up in some dangerous waters. That's why our daughters need initiative. And it is why it is so vitally important that we parents be countercultural, just as the parents of the Proverbs 31 Woman were.

"I know you can handle it."

When Reagan was very young, her favorite phrase was "I DO IT" in her childish voice of independence. She truly believed she could do anything. This confidence has carried on into her adult life. Recently our daughter Reagan showed up at our garage workbench with a big old pool pump valve she had removed from its mounting and wrestled into her car. She was fixing a handle on the pump, but she realized she needed to put it in a vise to finish the job. She didn't have a vise, which was why she came to me.

I know it's a small thing—and believe me, I've seen Reagan show initiative in plenty of much bigger things—but I was proud of my daughter for showing that kind of initiative. The pump needed fixing, so she rolled up her sleeves and got to fixing it. She didn't wait for somebody to take care of her; she took responsibility, took care of business. Her husband, John David, was out of town that day. When she called to tell him about the problem, he didn't say, "I'll take care of it when I get home." He didn't even say, "Call the pool repairman." He said, "I know you can handle it."

When I heard that, I thought about the husband of the Proverbs 31 Woman: "The heart of her husband safely trusts her" (v. 11 NKJV). He trusts in her because she shows initiative. She makes things happen. When John David got home from his trip, the pool pump was as good as new.

"You can do anything you want . . . if you want it bad enough."

I always told Reagan and Brodie what my father always told me: you can do whatever you want, if you want it bad enough. You might say that was the beginning of Big Oak Ranch. I was twenty-three and really didn't have a clue about raising boys or operating a ranch or running a business or raising money. I just knew I felt called to this work, and I figured if God called me to do it, He would give me what I needed to make it happen. After seeing the land, I sat in my car that first meeting with the owner of the property that is now the Boys' Ranch and simply said, "Lord, I'm willing." That's all he asks.

As I started Big Oak Ranch, I found that initiative is a delicate balance between being confident in my ability to do whatever task is in front of me and trusting God to make the whole thing happen. That phrase "confident in my ability" may be misleading. The whole thing, first and last, is confidence in God. Any ability I trusted in myself was ability that God had put there. God put the desire in me, and God put the ability in me. If it is true that you can do what you want "if you want it bad enough," it's because God puts the wanting there too.

> *I found that initiative is a delicate balance between being confident in my ability to do whatever task is in front of me and trusting God to make the whole thing happen.*

As we equip our daughters for life, it is vitally important that we pay attention to what they want—what they really, ultimately want (as we discussed in the chapter on righteousness), not what they think they want in that immediate time. That desire is more important even than talent or ability. Your daughter's talents are an important clue to understanding who God made her to be. But an even more important clue is the desire that he put in her. If your daughter is a gifted basketball player, that's great. But does she have a great desire to play basketball? If she's an okay dancer, but dance is what makes her come alive, you might consider saving your basketball team fees and investing in some dance lessons.

Now for a hard question: Do you know what your daughter wants? Sometimes it's hard to hear what our kids want because our own desires for our kids are barking so loudly. Of course you only want what's best for your daughter. But you have to be open to the possibility that what you want for your daughter may not actually be what she wants nor be what's best for her.

Once you have heard what your daughter wants, help her pursue it and succeed in it. Sign her up for those lessons. Let her join that team. But be careful not to push too hard. You need to check yourself: Is it her desire that is the driving force, or is it your desire?

Letting your daughter fail.

I do need to clarify one thing: to help your daughter to succeed isn't the same thing—isn't even close to the same thing—as protecting her from failure or disappointment. Protecting kids from disappointment is one of the biggest mistakes good parents make. They rig the deck so their kids can't lose. They fuss at the teacher when their kid makes a bad grade. They give everybody a trophy. But here's the thing: when your kids go out into the world, they're going to find out that the world isn't set up to let them win every time. The world still, and probably always will, reward people with initiative and skills. Wouldn't you prefer that they learn those lessons, suffer those disappointments, while they're still living in your house and you can walk them through it?

In the last few years child development experts have started talking a lot more about "resilience"—a person's ability to get back up after a disappointment. The "helicopter parenting" that solves every problem for a child and protects her from failure also makes it very hard for her to succeed. There is a kind of involved parenting that robs children of resiliency and, therefore, robs them of initiative.

What do you do when your daughter really wants to do something and you know she's going to fail at it? The temptation is to discourage her. You want to spare her the pain, and you want to spare yourself too. But to protect her from pain or even from embarrassment may be to rob her of initiative. You know from your own life that failure is sometimes the best thing that can happen to a person's character. I'm not talking, of course, about the kind of failure that leads to permanent damage. If your daughter's dream is to skydive without a parachute or to ride off with the Hell's Angels, by all means discourage those dreams.

We had a girl at the Ranch who desperately wanted to go to college. Everybody who knew her could see that she wasn't going to make it as a college student. Her gifts didn't lie in that direction. But we rounded up the tuition money and sent her to a nearby college. Before the first semester was over, she came back and said, "I can't do this." That was fine. We helped her find another path that didn't involve college. But it made all the difference in the world that she was the one who said, "I can't do this" rather than one of us saying, "You can't do this." She is now married and a mom to two wonderful children and doing great!

Or how about this: your daughter is four foot nothing. She loves basketball. You know she's never going to play basketball past high school, and she may not even manage to make the varsity team in high school. Do you discourage her? No way. She might turn out to be the greatest basketball coach ever. Great coaches, I've noticed, often weren't great players. But they have more passion for the game than many of the great players. And the fact that the game has never come easy for them means that they are real students of the game and, therefore, better able to teach it.

John Wooden wasn't a great basketball player. Bear Bryant wasn't a great football player. Ray Perkins, the head coach who followed Bear Bryant at Alabama, *was* a great player. He was an All-American wide receiver at Alabama, catching passes from Joe Namath. I'll never forget seeing him explain a particular route to a group of wide receivers. "You just run down ten yards, make the DB turn his hips, and then you've got him." Being one of those players, I gave him a blank look. Coach Perkins tried it again. "It's easy. Ten yards. The DB turns his hips. Then you've got him." I still didn't get it. So Coach Perkins ran the route himself to show us what he was talking about. We got it eventually, but it wasn't nearly as easy for us as it was for him. He didn't know what it was like *not* to be an All-American receiver. In coaching, as in so many things, desire is more important than talent. He was and is a great coach, having coached in the NFL and at the University of Alabama after Coach Bryant retired. But he had to learn to "dummy down" his instruction so we could understand.

Practical Helps and Suggestions

How do you encourage initiative in your daughter? You want your daughter to be like the Excellent Woman of Proverbs 31—the kind of woman who "kicks butt and takes names," not somebody who is waiting for somebody to take care of her, but somebody who is taking care of her business and taking care of other people. That's a matter of attitude, but it's also a matter of skill. It's important that you grow your daughter's confidence and initiative by enabling her to gain real skills in areas that she is passionate about. The point isn't necessarily that she will use specific skills later in life (she may or may not save the world by being, say, an excellent horsewoman), but that she will learn *how* to pursue her passions to excellence. That's one of the most important skills she can have.

Find out your daughter's passions.

Do you know what your daughter really cares about? Have you ever asked? Sit down with her and find out what her passions are. It is important that you separate your wishes from her passions.

Invest in your daughter's interests.

One way to show your daughter that you care about her interests is to commit to those interests. Sign her up for lessons. Drive her to practice. Go to her games. Practice *with* her when possible—shooting hoops, riding bikes, running a 5K together, etc. Whatever your daughter is invested in, make sure you are invested in it as well.

When possible, insist that your daughter invest financially too.

Ideally, your daughter should work for the things she cares about—and I don't mean she should just work hard at practice. Let her work for the money to pay part of the registration fee or the tuition. If your daughter is a gifted actress and you can send her to, say, the local school for the arts, help her get a job so she can make the money to pay part of the tuition. If it is important to her, she needs to have a little skin in the game. Anything freely given loses value.

When your daughter says, "Watch this!," watch.

Reagan was the kind of girl who couldn't play by herself even when she was playing by herself. She always wanted one of us to watch. When I took her swimming, every time she jumped off the diving board she would yell, "Watch!" You've seen parents who are so self-absorbed that they don't hear when their kid says, "Watch!" Or they watch distractedly. After four or five times of being ignored, a kid is going to stop saying "Watch!" when she jumps off the diving board. And then she's going to stop jumping off the diving board. You don't want to rob her of her initiative that way. She needs to hear you brag on her.

Let your daughter see you succeed.

I love "take your daughter to work" day. I think it's great for girls to see what their parents do. As I said earlier, I suspect that the Proverbs 31 Woman gained all those amazing skills at the ancient Israelite version of "take your daughter to work" day. Let her see you doing what you were built to do.

66

Let your daughter see you fail.

How do you handle failure? Your daughter needs to see you stretch yourself and try things that you aren't necessarily good at. In most ways, it's a parent's job to play it safe. But it's also important that your kids see you expand-ing your horizons and not playing it safe. Does that mean your daughter will see you fail? Probably so. It will be a good lesson for her.

> *Your daughter needs to see you stretch yourself and try things that you aren't necessarily good at.*

Don't stifle your daughter's initiative in the name of protecting her from failure.

Don't teach your daughter to be afraid to try things she might fail at. After failing over and over again to make a lightbulb, Thomas Edison is quoted as saying, "I have not failed. I have found 10,000 ways that won't work." Failure is a great teacher, especially when your daughter is still in your house, and you can walk her through the process of getting back up. When she's out on her own, the landing may not be so soft. Most teachers teach you the lesson before they give you the test. Life, on the other hand, gives you the test first and then teaches you the lesson.

Remember that praise makes your daughter keep trying.

In my years at Big Oak Ranch, I have been given some pretty bad drawings by some very sweet little girls. I have one picture that might be of a horse or might be a bowl of fruit. But I always praise the picture, for two reasons. First and most important, I praise the picture because it is always given out of love, and its artistic quality doesn't matter a penny compared to that. But second, I praise the picture so that the girl will keep on drawing. And when she draws the next picture, it will look a little more like a horse (or a fruit bowl, as the case may be). And the drawing after that one will be even better.

Don't let your daughter listen to a culture that tells her that women are just sex objects or materialistic bimbos.

Your daughter is constantly getting false messages from the world around her. You have to talk more loudly and more clearly than the culture, reassuring her that there are better things in store for her. Don't settle for the Kool-Aid of false promises from the world versus what you know is right and God instructs.

Remember that you aren't God.

You don't know what the future holds for your daughter any more than you could guess what will become of a tulip bulb if you didn't know already. Be open to what God has for her, and don't focus on imposing your own agenda.

Conclusion

I'm not too big on chick flicks, but I did see *The Notebook*, based on the Nicholas Sparks novel by the same name. It's a movie about a young woman whose initiative is crushed and then brought to life again. Allison is a vibrant and artistically talented young woman from a wealthy family. She loves a boy named Noah, but her parents don't approve because he's not from their social class.

Allison and Noah break up, and she ends up getting engaged to a man named Lon, who is a "better fit" from her parents' perspective (he's rich and upwardly mobile), but she doesn't love him like she loved Noah. One day it occurs to her that she hasn't drawn or painted a single picture since she has been engaged to Lon. She leaves him and goes back to Noah. And everybody in the audience knows she has made the right move when Noah surprises her with a gift: a set of paints, an easel, and a blank canvas.

Noah was in touch with the passions that gave Allison life. The other people in her life—her parents, her fiancé—were dream takers, but Noah brought her dream back. Her initiative came to life again.

How about you? Are you in touch with the passions and interests that give your daughter life and that make her the unique person whom God made her to be?

You are in the unique position to be your daughter's dream maker or dream taker. Your choices determine which one you will be.

Notes

1. Nosson Scherman, *The Complete Artscroll Siddur* (Mesorah Pubns Ltd, 1984).

Chapter 4

Nurture

 One day I came out of the office at the Girls' Ranch and saw a young woman with two little children. She seemed a little young to be a mother of two, but it was easy to see that she had the heart of a nurturer. She was extremely attentive to the children. As I held the door for the three of them, I told the young woman, "Your children are beautiful. You must be proud of them."

The young woman blushed and looked down. "Oh, these aren't my children," she said. "They're my brother and sister. I'm only fifteen years old."

She was only fifteen years old, but her circumstances required that she act as the mother for her two siblings. For over three years, her nurturing muscles had grown strong.

And do you know what? It made a woman of her, even though she was still a girl.

Seeing that woman-child made me think of a kitchen trick I've heard about. If you want to speed up the ripening of unripe fruit, you can put it in a paper sack with a banana. Bananas give off some kind of chemical called ethylene that triggers maturation in other fruits. The act of nurturing is like those bananas. When a young girl gets in the habit of nurturing, the other fruits in her life begin to mature. Love, joy, peace, forbearance, kindness, goodness, faithfulness, gentleness and self-control—all of these fruits of the Spirit grow in a girl who grows in nurture. That's why I mistook that fifteen-year-old girl for a young mother.

> *Love, joy, peace, forbearance, kindness, goodness, faithfulness, gentleness, and self-control—all of these fruits of the Spirit grow in a girl who grows in nurture.*

I often hear parents say that their daughters are growing up too fast. That may be true. But some of what we call "growing up too fast" is actually a matter of not growing up fast enough. God intends for our girls to grow up in spiritual and emotional maturity and wisdom—and to grow up faster in those areas than many parents seem to expect their daughters to. In our culture, kids are exposed to so much that eleven-year-olds are like fifteen-year-olds; but then, when they're twenty, they're still like fifteen-year-olds!

Nurture is something that moves our daughters down the track toward maturity. You see it in the way a little girl takes care of a baby doll or a puppy. You see it in the way a big sister takes care of siblings. You see it in the way a middle-school girl takes responsibility for the kids she babysits. And in the teenage years, when girls can get especially selfish, nurture pulls them out of themselves.

Nurture is a central fact of womanhood. When a little boy falls down and hurts himself, who does he call for? It's not Daddy. Oh, Daddy will do if Mama's not around, but Daddy is the junior varsity. The varsity, the first-string, is Mama. When a kid needs comfort and nurture, it's mama he wants. On my best day, I'm still not the nurturer that my wife is on her worst day. It's just the way God made us.

The point I'm making here is that a nurturing spirit comes more naturally for girls and women. It's God-given. I have definitely seen women for whom that nurturing spirit has been broken. Their children often end up at the Ranch. It's interesting to see how that plays out in those women's daughters. Some girls, like that fifteen-year-old I mentioned earlier, step up and become the nurturer. Others, because

> *We as parents still need to create a nurturing environment in which our daughters will be able to grow into nurturers themselves.*

they don't have a model to learn how to nurture, turn out to be as broken in that area as their mothers. In any case, I'm convinced that there is at least a seed of nurture that God put in every girl. We as parents still need to create a nurturing environment in which our daughters will be able to grow into nurturers themselves. In other words, we need to nurture a spirit of nurturing.

The Nurturing Spirit of the Proverbs 31 Woman

If you wonder about the Proverbs 31 Woman's ability to nurture, consider one verse: "Her children rise up and call her blessed" (v. 28). There's the reward for her love and nurture. She has blessed her children, and now they bless her.

Look at the verses that lead up to the children's blessing: "She opens her mouth with wisdom, and the teaching of kindness is on her tongue." The language here describes a woman who is gently leading her children—teaching not just with wisdom, but with kindness. She created an environment in which her children were able to thrive and grow. "She looks well to the ways of her household," verse 27 says. That's another way of saying that she is nurturing. Again, she's creating a safe environment for growth. Her children thrive—and why? Because she thrives. We have already seen what a capable woman the Proverbs 31 Woman must have been. She was nurtured, and now she is nurturing.

I have often said that you judge a man's parenting by his grandchildren. Did he raise his children in such a way that they were equipped to carry on his principles of love and commitment to the next generation? As you nurture your daughter, you are preparing her to nurture her daughters and sons—your grandchildren.

It's not just the children of the Proverbs 31 Woman who bless her. Her husband has been the recipient of her nurture as well, and he blesses her for it: "Many women have done excellently, but you surpass them all" (v. 29). There's more to godly nurture than the nurture of children. A godly wife and mother will also nurture her husband.

Consider Genesis 2:24: "Therefore a man shall leave his father and his mother and hold fast to his wife, and they shall become one flesh." Notice anything strange about that verse? God only commands about the *man* leaving his mother and father. Why doesn't he say anything about the woman leaving her mother and father too? I think it's because nobody has to tell a woman to leave and cleave. For a woman, it's the most natural thing in the world. She wants to create a space where she can begin nurturing her own people. The man, on the other hand—he's used to being nurtured. He has to be pushed out of the nest, so to speak, so he will leave behind the nurture of his old family and join with his wife to create a new environment of nurture.

There's one other thing I want to point out about the Bible's view of motherly nurture. It's one of the ways that God uses to explain his own love and care for his people. In Luke 13:34, Jesus speaks tenderly to the people of Jerusalem, who have a well-deserved reputation for killing and rejecting the prophets of God. He might have lashed out at them in anger; who could blame him? Instead, this is what Jesus said: "O Jerusalem, Jerusalem, the city that kills the prophets and stones those who are sent to it! How often would I have gathered your children together as a hen gathers her brood under her wings, and you were not willing!" The nurture of a mother (in this case, a mother hen) is a picture of Jesus' love for us. In spite of the rebelliousness of the people of Jerusalem (and in spite of our rebelliousness), Jesus longs to gather them (and us) up like a mother hen gathers up her chicks and protects them from the dangers of the world.

But nurture isn't all sweetness. Sometimes a nurturer is tougher than nails. I call it the Mama Bear Syndrome. In

Hosea 13, when God wanted to describe his fierceness in judging rebellious sinners, notice the images he uses:

> So I will be like a lion to them;
> Like a leopard I will lie in wait by the wayside.
> I will encounter them like a bear robbed of her cubs,
> And I will tear open their chests;
> There I will also devour them like a lioness,
> As a wild beast would tear them. (Hosea 13:7–8 NASB)

A lion and a leopard are pretty tough. But as it turns out, they're just the warm-up act. Things get really serious when God compares himself to "a bear robbed of her cubs" and "a lioness." The Mama Bear Syndrome is real. It's just the flip side of the nurture coin.

Sometimes a nurturer is tougher than nails.

Two Sides of Nurturing

For every girl who comes to the Ranch with her nurture muscles strengthened by hardship, there's a girl who comes to the Ranch whose nurture muscles are shredded. Nurture has never been modeled for them, and they don't know how to do it.

My wife Tee is a nurturer. She would do anything for Reagan and Brodie, our son. She nurtures me too. She's the kind of person who feels another person's hurt. She would do anything to soothe the hurt of one of her loved ones— that is, unless the hurt turns out to be exactly what her loved one needs.

I'll give you an example. I've had both knees replaced in the last couple of years. Tee's sense of empathy is so strong that sometimes it seemed like she felt more pain during my recovery than I did. She winced every time I took a limping step on my new knees. But when it was time to do my physical therapy, she got me up and made me do it, whether I wanted to or not. If you've ever had physical therapy after surgery, you know how much it hurts. It's easier to stay in the La-Z-Boy, watch another game, and hope the knee loosens up on its own. That would have been easier and less painful, but it would have been exactly what I didn't need. So she coaxed me up and got me going.

And here's the thing: even though *she* was the one who wouldn't let me quit on my therapy, even though she was the one who cajoled me out of the chair, she sat there in the therapy room and hurt just as much to see me in such pain. That's a perfect picture of what nurture looks like in the real world. It sometimes needs to be tough, but it's incredibly empathetic.

Ezer Kenegdo

There's a phrase from Genesis describing Eve that is usually translated "help meet" or sometimes "helpmate" or "helper." The phrase is *ezer kenegdo*. Stasi Eldredge writes about this phrase at some length in *Captivating*, a book she wrote with her husband, John Eldredge.

That translation—"helper" or "help meet"—does paint a picture of a woman who's there to support and be of assistance and generally make life easier for the man in her life. But I'm not sure that's a very complete picture of what God has in mind for wives and mothers.

The Hebrew scholar Robert Alter translates that phrase *ezer kenegdo* as "sustainer beside him." The word *kenegdo* means something like "alongside." But that word *ezer* is pretty special. Every other time it is used in the Bible, it is used to describe God himself. Specifically, it is used to describe God in those moments when we desperately need him.

As Eldredge writes in *Captivating*, "Most of these contexts are life and death and God is your only hope. Your 'ezer.' If he is not there beside you . . . you are dead. A better translation therefore of 'ezer' would be 'lifesaver.'"[1] A wife and mother isn't just a meek helper. She's working alongside her husband so that they can do incredible things together. In addition, Stasi Eldredge wrote in *Captivating*:

The life God calls us to is not a safe life. God calls us to a life involving frequent risks and many dangers. Why else would we need him to be our "ezer"? You don't need a lifesaver if your mission is to be a couch potato. You need an "ezer" when your life is in constant danger.

That longing in the heart of a woman to share life together as a great adventure—that comes straight from the heart of God . . . Eve is essential. She has an irreplaceable role to play. And so you'll see that women are endowed with fierce devotion, an ability to suffer great hardships, a vision to make the world a better place.[2]

In my heart, I *know* we are in a battle for the souls of our children. The enemy is strong and well-equipped. If I could expand on *ezer kenegdo,* I would describe a wife as a "warrior beside." Now *that's* a wife of worth! Every woman of worth that I know yearns to have this position beside her man. We must teach our daughters to have this kind of heart.

> *In my heart, I know we are in a battle for the souls of our children.*

We've already talked about the Mama Bear Syndrome that is the flip side of nurturing. But the nurturing heart of a woman is even more complex than that. As you build on your daughter's nurturing instincts, you are preparing her to be a mighty warrior. It seems counterintuitive, doesn't it? The Bible often is.

Male Nurture?

We men have a certain amount of nurture in us; I don't mean to suggest that only women have the nurturing gene. And we men do have an important role to play in helping our daughters to become nurturers themselves. But our way of nurturing and protecting tends to be very different from that of our wives.

I remember once when we had just moved into our current house, we had a new alarm system that we hadn't quite gotten the hang of—or maybe it hadn't gotten the hang of us. Anyway, one night Tee and I were sleeping soundly in our room and the kids in theirs when the alarm started screeching, "INTRUDER FRONT DOOR! INTRUDER FRONT DOOR!" Not what you want to hear in the middle of the night.

I sprang out of bed and ran to the front door. When I got there, I jerked the door open and there was no one there. Frankly, I was disappointed because my adrenaline level was off the charts. Everyone who has been in a similar situation knows that feeling.

I returned to our bedroom and Tee was nowhere to be found. I said to myself, "I'm out here fighting the bad guys, and she's gone!" I hollered, "Where are you?" And she answered, "Up here with the kids."

She never once thought of getting to the front door. She had only one agenda—get to my children! Tee wasn't hiding from the intruder. When I headed toward the front door, she headed straight to the kids' rooms. I was protecting the family in my way, and she was protecting the family in her way. If there actually had been an intruder, and if he had gotten past me and my baseball bat, he would have had to face Tee. From the leopard to the mama bear, as Hosea put it. I wouldn't have liked his chances.

Practical Helps and Suggestions

If nurture is innate for girls and women, how do you make it grow? Broadly speaking, the way you grow a nurturing spirit in your daughter is to nurture her. Model nurture and you will find that your daughter learns nurture. Here are a few more specific suggestions for growing and encouraging the seed of the nurturing spirit in your daughter.

As appropriate, and as early as possible, give your daughter opportunities to care for others.

She's going to do it anyway. She's going to tuck her baby dolls in. She's going to play mother to her brother who just wants to be left alone. Reagan used to drive Brodie crazy trying to be his second mama. My first inclination was always to tell her to leave the poor guy alone. I know I wouldn't enjoy being mothered to death if I were in his shoes. One mama was enough, and I would hate for his growth toward manhood to be stunted by too much coddling. But usually I managed to stop myself. The nurturing by Reagan wasn't really going to interfere with Brodie's growth toward independence and manhood, and it *was* a key part of Reagan's growth toward being a godly woman. She needed to nurture in order to grow into the person God made her to be. She now is an incredible nurturer to her husband and three boys—and as Childcare Team Director at the Ranch, to *all* of the children who call Big Oak Ranch their home. Reagan is the best I know at what she does for our children.

You can leverage your daughter's natural nurturing behavior by giving her little tasks that require her to be nurturing. Ask her to feed her baby brother while you finish up some dishes. Give that young mother down the street a break and keep her baby for an afternoon, then let your daughter participate in the care of the baby. Give your daughter the opportunity to care for an elderly friend at church. Be creative here.

Get your daughter a pet to take care of.

At Big Oak Ranch, we have found that one of the best ways to build habits of nurture in a little girl is to get her involved in horses. Girls love horses, and especially ponies.

> *You can leverage your daughter's natural nurturing behavior by giving her little tasks that require her to be nurturing.*

For a girl to have an animal that depends completely on her the way a horse does can have a transforming effect. I see it over and over again at the Ranch. A girl who has a pet always has a friend. But also—and this is a very important point—she is solely responsible for taking care of that friend. The combination of responsibility on the one hand, and on the other hand a real desire to carry out that responsibility, motivated by love—that's as good a lesson on what it means to be a nurturer as you could hope for.

I realize that not everybody is in a position to get a horse or a big, slobbery Labrador. Some people live in apartments where pets aren't allowed. Some people have allergies. If you have to get a couple of goldfish in a bowl instead of a dog or a cat, you can make that work. I do think that a mammal is probably the better choice if you're trying to develop

NURTURE

nurturing skills; there's a limit to how much you can cuddle a goldfish or a turtle.

Again, I know that horses and dogs and cats aren't right for every family. But if you have been resistant to getting a pet, I am pointing out some of the advantages from a child-raising (and especially a daughter-raising) perspective. And I suppose I'm challenging you to examine your reasons for being resistant to getting a pet for your daughter to love and be responsible for.

Watch for nurturing behavior in your daughter and reward it. But also help her be wise.

I have a friend whose daughter got in the car in the school carpool line one cold winter's day without her coat. "Where's your coat?" she asked the girl.

"My coat?" her daughter answered. "Oh, um, I left it in my classroom."

"Well," my friend said, "you'd better go get it. It's cold today."

The girl looked down at her hands. "Um . . . Mom . . . my coat isn't in the classroom. I gave it away. There was a girl in my class who didn't have a coat, and I gave her mine. I have others at home that I can wear, and she didn't have one at all."

That's the kind of nurture we're looking for in our girls. The cost of a coat? That's a pretty small price to pay for the

85

kind of character and compassion that this girl showed. My friend took a minute right there in the carpool line to tell her daughter how proud she was of her giving spirit.

Later in the day, the daughter and mother had another conversation about the coat. "Sweetie," my friend said, "like I said earlier, I am so very proud of your willingness to give up your coat for a girl who needed one. That unselfishness is the most important thing. But can I be a part of the process next time? That coat was special ordered for you, and it had your initials embroidered on it. Next time, it might be best if you talk it over with me before you give your coat away, and we can decide which one is best to give away, or maybe we'll decide it's best to go buy your friend a new coat."

> *Be alert. Watch for the signs of a nurturing spirit in your daughter and praise and encourage her in it.*

Be alert. Watch for the signs of a nurturing spirit in your daughter and praise and encourage her in it. But also help her navigate the sometimes tricky path of helping in ways that are most helpful.

For dads only: take care of your wives.

The quickest way to create exhaustion is to try to nurture others when you don't feel cared for yourself. Whenever I see a mother who looks exhausted and run down, my first question is: What is her husband doing to build her up? Great men I know help their wives. I see many married women who are single moms, if you know what I mean.

Men, your wives care for your families out of reservoirs that you can help fill. Your wife needs to know that you're on her side. She needs to know that she's your *ezer kenegdo*, fighting the good fight alongside you. Speak words of praise to your wife—not occasionally, but every day. She needs to know that the work she's doing is worthwhile. And she needs practical help as well. It's not going to kill you to do dishes or take a turn with the laundry. It's amazing to me that there are men who come home after putting in a full day of work at the office, put their feet up, and expect to be served hand and foot by a wife who has also put in a full day of work at the office!

If your daughter sees a mother who is exhausted and spent and bitter from trying to nurture her family alone, that's not exactly a motivator for her to be a nurturer herself. You and your wife are a team. Of course you'll have different roles within the team. But your role isn't simply to be on the receiving end of your wife's nurture and hard work. Your role includes giving her what she needs to be able to keep nurturing with a cheerful heart.

Help your daughter see the difference between being a nurturer and being a doormat.

It takes strength to be a nurturer. It also takes vision. A doormat is always doing another person's bidding, subject to that person's whims. A nurturer says, "I know what you need, and I'm going to take care of that for you." A doormat does whatever it takes to make the other person happy or to avoid conflict. A nurturer says, "If you're not happy right this minute—or if you're not happy with me—I'm okay with that. I want you to be happy and do what's best for you in the long run."

Help your daughter understand that people pleasing isn't on the nurturer's agenda. We'll talk more about this idea in the upcoming chapter on servant-heartedness. This isn't an easy concept for a girl to grasp. But if you can help her to grasp it, you will protect her from becoming a doormat and put her on the path toward strong nurture.

Conclusion

A few years back, we got a new little girl at the Ranch, ten years old. On the first night in her new home, her house-mom tucked her in bed and helped her say her prayers.

Before she flipped off the light, the little girl said, "Thank you, thank you, thank you."

"Thank you for what?" the housemom asked.

"Thank you for tucking me in. I've never had anybody tuck me in, and I've always dreamed about being tucked in someday."

Tears welled up in the housemom's eyes to think about a little girl whose biggest wish was as simple as being tucked in, and who had never even seen that modest wish fulfilled in ten years.

"Oh, honey," the housemom said. "That's just what mamas do. You have a mama now. You can expect a lot of tucking-in."

That little girl, who had experienced so much hurt and loneliness in her first ten years, thrived under the nurture that she was given by that housemom.

A while back I was flipping through the channels and I was struck by the contrast between two different television shows that were airing at the same time. On one channel was "Real Housewives of *some major city*," whatever city they decided to do that year. If you haven't seen the show, it is a reality show about women who seem to spend all their time shopping and eating lunch and getting their nails done. They have kids, but they hire nannies to take care of them. The kids whine at the "real housewives," and the "real housewives" buy them stuff or let them do what they want so they'll quit whining. The "real housewives" have husbands, but their idea of being a good wife seems to be having plastic surgery in order to change the way they look. There was plenty of pampering going on, but it was directed at the women. They were the receivers of pampering when they should have been the givers of nurture.

On the next channel was a documentary about refugees somewhere in Africa. There I saw a very different kind of mother. I saw a mother who was stick-thin from malnutrition, and on her back she carried a toddler who was almost as thin as she was. She had been carrying her baby for twenty-one days across the desert to try to get to a refugee camp across the border of her war-torn country. When she staggered into the camp, she handed her child off to the first Red Cross worker she saw. Then she collapsed at his feet. That's nurture. She did what she had to do to take care of that baby. She gave of herself—every bit of herself—to give her child the opportunity to survive and thrive. And one of these days, that child is going to rise up and call her blessed.

Notes

1. John Eldredge and Stasi Eldredge, *Captivating* (Nashville, TN: Thomas Nelson Publishers, 2005, 2010).
2. Ibid.

Chapter 5

Character

 The career of the famous racehorse Seabiscuit didn't begin with a great start. He had impressive genetics: his grandsire was the legendary Man O'War. But Seabiscuit was very different from his grandsire. Actually, he was very different from almost any other Thoroughbred in the world. Instead of being tall and graceful, he was short and knobby-kneed. And whereas Thoroughbreds tend to be high-strung, Seabiscuit was about as laid-back as an old Labrador.

Horses typically sleep standing up, in lots of naps that only last a few minutes each. Not Seabiscuit. He would lie down in his stable and snooze for hours and hours, late into the morning. All the other horses would have been up, eaten breakfast, and headed out to train, and the trainers would have to come to Seabiscuit's stable to wake him up.

When it came to his actual performance on the race track, Seabiscuit wasn't exactly slow, but he wasn't nearly the performer that his pedigree would lead you to expect. He didn't at all look like he was cut from the same cloth as Man O' War. Seabiscuit's first owner came to expect less and less of him and focused more time and training resources on his stable mates. Everybody was convinced that Seabiscuit was just lazy.

At a race in Massachusetts, a trainer named Tom Smith watched Seabiscuit win a race, and he saw tremendous potential in the horse. He spoke to his boss Charles Howard, an automotive millionaire and racehorse owner, and said, "Get me that horse. He has real stuff in him. I can improve him. I'm positive."

Howard bought Seabiscuit for $8000, and Smith devoted himself to helping the horse reach his potential. Sensitive to the damage Seabiscuit had suffered from neglect at his previous stable, Smith nurtured him, letting him sleep as much as he liked and—strangely enough—giving him a dog, a monkey, and another horse to keep him company in an extra-large stall. Smith nurtured Seabiscuit, but he didn't spoil him. He worked him hard and, for the first time, Seabiscuit responded to his training. Within two years, he had become the top racehorse in America.

What does the story of a talented but lazy and undisciplined horse have to do with character? Simply this: a woman of character is a woman who is living as the person God made her to be. But we all need nurture and training to be that person.

A racehorse is made to run. He is happiest when he is running. If you've ever watched a horse race, those Thoroughbreds look like they're smiling all the way around the track. But a racehorse still needs a bit and bridle. Left to his own devices, Seabiscuit was lazy and undisciplined. He was also miserable. Tom Smith helped Seabiscuit to live out his purpose. He helped him live out his true character. And it seemed nothing made Seabiscuit happier.

Character requires training and discipline.

As we help our daughters grow into women of character, we are training them to find fulfillment in becoming the women God made them to be. Character requires training and discipline. But we run into trouble when we think of discipline as a means of training a person into something she's not. It's more helpful, I believe, to think of discipline as a means of training a person into whom she truly is.

Seabiscuit was a great racehorse. Tom Smith didn't change Seabiscuit from a mediocre racehorse into a great one. He released Seabiscuit to live out what was true about him all along.

Character is choice. Character is choosing what you *really* want and not being distracted by smaller, temporary desires. Let me change the image from racehorses to bird dogs. Consider how a bird dog works. He is made to point up (find) quail. He's bred for it and trained for it. Nothing makes him happier than pointing up (or finding) a covey of quail. When he's in the field and a rabbit appears, he has a choice to make. Is he going to chase the rabbit, or is he going to continue hunting birds? He may be highly trained and well-bred, but he's still a dog, and dogs love to chase rabbits. Will he choose that petty desire, or will he choose to be the dog he was made to be—the dog who is most pleasing to his master?

Sometimes we think of character as the ability to choose *against* your desires: you feel like misbehaving, but you choose to be good instead. That's only partly true. I think it's better to say that character is the ability to ignore your petty desires in your pursuit of your bigger desires. You want to eat a fistful of Twinkies, and you are strongly tempted to do so, but you also want to be slim and healthy. A person of character chooses not to eat the Twinkies. Is she choosing against her desires? Well, sort of. But in the big picture, she is actually choosing *according to* her desires.

We touched on this in the chapter on righteousness. Helping your daughter to be righteous, or a person of character, means helping her see what she really wants. The difference between righteousness and character, at least in the way I'm using the terms, is the difference between general and specific. We spoke of righteousness as walking tall and straight in a world of limpers—living by God's normality rather than the world's normality. Building character starts with recognizing your calling, then pursuing that calling.

A few years ago Max Lucado wrote a book called *Living in Your Sweet Spot*. That's a good way of expressing what I'm talking about. Once your daughter discovers her "sweet spot," the purpose God made her for, she's going to find that living there makes her more effective in every-

> *Building character starts with recognizing your calling, then pursuing that calling.*

thing she does. There's more to character than "living in your sweet spot" or working effectively. But I have found that when people are living out their calling, they are less inclined to the kinds of behavior we associate with weak character—the shortcuts, the little white lies, etc. People who have purpose live character-filled lives.

The Character of the Excellent Woman

Nearly every Tuesday morning during the school year, I have breakfast with all of the high school boys at 7:00 a.m. and the high school girls at 7:30 a.m. The kids call it "Breakfast with Mr. John."

Our time together is simply us talking about "stuff." Sometimes very serious and sometimes light and fun. There's always a lesson, whether it's subtle or direct.

We had a little girl named Jerri who would help clean up the tables after everyone had gone to class. She has already arranged with her block instructor to be a few minutes late. I asked her why, and she said, "It's not right to leave a mess for the lunchroom staff to clean up."

Some of you might feel this story should be in the upcoming servant-heartedness chapter, but I believe her reason outshines her service. Look at what she said—"It's *not* right . . ." These three words sum up character—doing what's right even when no one else is doing it.

The Character of Rahab

Strangely enough, one of the Bible's most vivid portraits of character is a prostitute. Rahab of Jericho had obviously made some bad choices, or she wouldn't have ended up a prostitute. On the other hand, however, we don't know what her options were. The Bible doesn't say what choices landed her in that situation. But it does tell us what choice she made and why she made it when she was confronted with the people of God.

You probably know Rahab's story already. When the Israelite spies came to Jericho in preparation for an invasion, they ended up at Rahab's house. Rahab had a choice. She could help the Israelites and protect them, or she could hand them over to the soldiers of Jericho who wanted to kill them. Her choice was between an old way of life and a new one.

Whatever had led Rahab into prostitution, she didn't want it any more. She wanted something better for herself. Also, she wanted something better for her family. So she struck a deal with the Israelites: "Now then, please swear to me by the LORD that, as I have dealt kindly with you, you also will deal kindly with my father's house, and give me a sure sign that you will save alive my father and mother, my brothers and sisters, and all who belong to them, and deliver our lives from death" (Josh. 2:12–13). See what is happening here? Rahab has a new sense of purpose. So she chooses accordingly. Also, she values her family. Her choice includes them too.

When the Israelites came back to destroy Jericho, they spared Rahab and her family. More than that, the Israelites welcomed this woman of character into the fold. In spite of her past, neither the Israelites nor God accepted her grudgingly. Rahab married an Israelite man and had children, who had children who had children. Her great-great grandson was none other than King David. This means she was also an ancestor of Jesus! Rahab showed that it's never too late to become a person of character, and that God rewards those who do.

Desire, Choice, Consequence

Character is about choices. Choices are about desires. We choose according to what we want most at the moment of choosing. And every choice has consequences, which may change the options for the next round of choices. A businessman who chooses to cheat his customer, for instance, may find that he doesn't have the same choices the next time around. He was free to cheat his customer the first time, but if his cheating costs him a customer, or if that customer starts spreading the word about the businessman's dishonest practices, the businessman's choices are limited by a new set of circumstances. If he ends up going to court over his dishonesty, that may mean a whole new set of limitations!

To say the same thing in a shorter form: *Choices create circumstances; decisions determine your future.*

A Framework for Decision-Making

When you help your daughter understand who she was made to be, you are giving her a framework for making choices. What are you communicating about what is most important? If having money is the most important thing in the world, if that's what you feel that you were made for, you will make a certain

> *Choices create circumstances; decisions determine your future.*

set of choices. On the other hand, if you feel that the most important thing in life is to play a role in the good things that God is doing to redeem the world, you will make a completely different set of choices.

You understand your place in the world (your calling), and you choose accordingly. That's character in a nutshell. We speak of people who "lack character." That's not technically accurate. Nobody "lacks" character. They may have bad character or weak character or strong character. But everybody chooses according to their moral framework—according to what they want and feel is most important at the moment of choosing. Your daughter may not have bad character, but if she has weak character, that can be just as bad in a tough situation. An example of the difference between weak character and strong character is a girl who gets in the backseat with a boy because she didn't want to tell him "no," as opposed to a girl who has decided to say "no" before the situation even arose.

Make sure that your daughter has strong enough character that there is no doubt what she will say when a tough situation arises.

Training is always at the core of parenting and preparing our daughters for the battle. Good training normally means good results. Bad training—or no training—almost always leads to bad results.

Practical Helps and Suggestions

Have you ever seen footage of spawning salmon swimming up a mountain river? It's hard work. The salmon are exhausted. And when they get to the hardest part—the rapids—the bears are waiting to swat them onto the bank and eat them. It doesn't seem quite fair. If only those salmon had some guidance, somebody to tell them where the bears *aren't*, somebody to tell them to keep to the left, where they can get up the rapids without having to jump out of the water and expose themselves.

> *Training is always at the core of parenting and preparing our daughters for the battle.*

If your daughter is a person of character, she's going to feel like one of those salmon. She's going to be swimming against the current all the time. And it is going to be tiring. She needs you there to support and strengthen her. She needs you to remind her that the struggle is worth it. Sometimes she will need you to push her along. But she needs a little more than that. She needs your help to avoid the bears. Here are some ways to help steer her through the rapids.

Know your daughter's friends.

Next to you and your spouse, your daughter's five best friends are the most influential people in her life. You need to know those five friends. You cannot control your daughter's friends, but you should know what kind of people she is running with. Invite them over for ice cream and game nights. When your daughter has friends over, make sure you spend some time with them; don't just let them disappear into another room the whole time they're there.

Once, Reagan wanted to go to a high school football game in North Alabama. She and her friends weren't old enough to drive yet, so I drove them to the game. I spoke very few words but listened intently to their "jabbering." Needless to say, I learned a lot! Spend as much time with them as you can. This not only allows you to get to know her friends but also creates a bonding experience with you and your daughter.

Give your daughter opportunities to make choices that have actual consequences.

If character is about choices, it's important that your daughter get some practice making choices. There are lots of things that you have to decide for her. You're going to decide where she goes to elementary through high school, where she goes to church, how much allowance you give her, etc. But as she grows, be aware of the decisions that you can let her make instead of making them for her. I'm not just talking about whether she drinks out of a blue cup or a yellow cup. I'm talking about choices that have consequences. It is extremely important that your daughter, from a very young age, begins to associate her choices with the consequences that result from those choices.

Take bedtime as an example. During the school week it's probably best that you choose your daughter's bedtime for her. But on Friday night (depending on your daughter's age), you might consider letting her decide what time she goes to bed. But (and this is a big *but*) you need to let your daughter live with the consequences of the bedtime she chooses. If she chooses a late bedtime, that doesn't mean she gets to sleep late. It doesn't mean she doesn't have to complete the chores you expect her to complete on Saturday morning. If your daughter chooses to stay up until midnight on Friday night, it might affect her performance at her 8:00 a.m.

soccer game on Saturday. As a parent, you need to be willing to let her live with those consequences.

There are two things that your daughter learns when you let her choose:

- She learns that she has independence.
- She learns that choices have consequences.

By "independence" I simply mean the power to make her own choices and make an impact on the world around her. Let's break down the word "independence." Take the root word *dependence* and place or direct it "in"—she has been trained to depend on herself because of training and practice.

> *As a parent, you need to be willing to let her live with those consequences.*

A person with this trait is a person who doesn't have life dictated to her, who doesn't simply have to take what the world gives her. Again, I'm not suggesting that your young daughter should have full independence or even feel that she has full independence. You're still the parent, and you need to make the most important choices in her life. But where can you let her make choices?

And the flip side of independence is consequence, both good and bad. A person with independence can make good things happen for her and others, or she can make bad or painful things happen for herself and others. Unless the consequences of your daughter's choices are genuinely harmful (and not just temporarily painful), it is important that you let those consequences play out. Without the consequences, good and bad, you can't teach independence. This leads me to my next point.

When your daughter makes poor choices, don't rescue her from the consequences.

It is our instinct as parents to protect our children. That's a good, God-given instinct. But protecting our children from real danger and real harm isn't the same thing as protecting them from all pain. They need to feel the painful consequences of bad choices while they're young and while they still have you there to help them recover. If you rescue your kids from the consequences of their actions—if you call the teacher to get that zero removed from the grade book or clean up her room for her while she naps in the aftermath of a sleepover—you aren't protecting her. You're putting her in harm's way.

I read a story about a student named Larry. He went out one Friday night and got rip-roaring drunk. He stumbled in at 2:00 a.m. and fell into bed, thinking that his parents didn't know what he had done.

At 6:00 a.m. that morning, Larry's dad turned on the lights and nudged him awake. "Late night last night," he said. "Were you drinking?"

Larry's head was splitting, and the room was spinning, and it was all he could do to form a sentence without throwing up. "No, Dad," he lied. "Of course not."

"Good," his father said. "Then you won't have any problem mowing your grandmother's yard this morning like you said you would." He then bundled Larry into the car, green face and all, drove him across town to his grandmother's hilly acre, and left him there with a push mower, a gas can, and two gallons of water. The temperature was well into the nineties before Larry finished the job. He says it was the worst morning of his life.

It was also the last time he ever got drunk.

Later that day, Larry's father gave him a lecture about the dangers of drinking. He told him that his body was a temple, and he quoted Bible verses about the foolishness of drunkards. The lecture was good and necessary. But mowing in the July heat with a hangover—that's what really inspired Larry's new, lifelong commitment to temperance. His father was a man who knew something about building character by letting his son experience real consequences for bad decisions.

Help your daughter to listen to her intuition.

You've heard the phrase "women's intuition." One of the gifts God gives to girls and women is the ability to feel when something isn't quite right about a situation or a person.

Let's say your daughter is going to a movie with a date and it turns out to be much worse than the boy described (whether intentional or not). Your daughter has a character choice to make. She can tell him, "I feel very uncomfortable with this movie. Can we leave?" *or* she can sit there and compromise her character. She is at a crossroads.

My wife and I have literally gotten up and left a movie more than once because we both felt we were compromising on a character choice.

If your daughter makes the right decision and her date says she's right and takes her out of the movie with no questions asked, maybe he has got something to him. *If* he makes fun of her and is not worried about her feelings, she needs to drop him like a bad habit because that is exactly what he is!

Your daughter has an innate radar for detecting when somebody is trying to get her to do something that isn't right. If she has been raised in a God-fearing home, she's going to feel a certain discomfort in those situations. People of good character pay attention to that discomfort. They listen to it and follow its advice. People of weak character are people who have learned to override that little check in their spirit.

One other thing I should mention on this subject: you need to help your daughter be realistic about life's dangers. Girls from good families sometimes don't realize that there are people in the world who can hurt them. They've always been protected, so how could they understand? But you know that the boyfriend who cusses her now is going to verbally abuse her later. The boyfriend who hits her probably isn't going to straighten up. Or if he does straighten up, it will be after she has sent him packing and he decides to treat his next girlfriend better. In the previous section I talked about protecting your daughter from real danger, not from the temporary pain of bad choices. That's what we're talking about here: real danger. I don't care how grown-up your daughter seems or how much she rolls her eyes at you; she doesn't have as much life-experience as you do, and she needs your protection and your training to spot these all-too-common situations.

If there is a growing distance between you and your daughter, find out why. And do something about it.

While her character is in its formative stages, your daughter needs you by her side. If she's not right there by your side, if it is becoming clear that she can't (or won't) talk to you, find out why immediately. It's true that, developmentally speaking, it is normal for adolescent girls and boys to separate somewhat from their parents. But holing up in her room from the minute she comes home, keeping ear buds constantly in her ears so she doesn't have to talk or listen, giving only one-word answers to your questions—those aren't things we should accept as normal.

What are possible reasons for distance between you and your daughter?

- Perhaps you have not been attentive to her. Children give up trying to communicate with their parents when they don't believe their parents are interested in communicating with them.

- Perhaps you have caused your daughter to feel shame. Few parents set out to shame their children. When we shame our children, it is usually because we feel fear. We're so worried that they're going to head down a wrong path that we try to shame them into walking on the right path. But in Christ, God has rescued us from both fear and shame.

- Perhaps your daughter feels guilt. Guilt isn't the same thing as shame. To feel shame is to feel that there is something wrong with me. Guilt, on the other hand, is what I feel when I have actually done something wrong. Guilt is a perfectly appropriate response when you realize that you have done wrong. But it can easily lead to shame. If your daughter is avoiding you because she feels guilt over something she has done wrong, you need to reach out to her. Help her to understand that there is forgiveness, and that she can be free from that guilt by repenting of her wrongdoing and receiving the grace that God promises through Christ. To me, the most important verse in the Bible ends with "I will not remember your sins" (Isa. 43:25). Remember that if you tell her

> *Remember that if you tell her she's forgiven, then don't keep bringing up the same issue over and over.*

she's forgiven, then *don't* keep bringing up the same issue over and over. I promise you this *will* lead to separation and bitterness. God has forgiven her. You would be wise to do the same.

Conclusion

We started this chapter with Seabiscuit. I want to end it with the other most famous racehorse of the twentieth century: Secretariat. In 1973, Secretariat won the Triple Crown—the Kentucky Derby, the Preakness Stakes, and the Belmont Stakes. Only eight horses had ever won these three races before. When he won that third race, he won it by thirty-one lengths! No horse had ever done that before. There's a famous picture of Secretariat coming down the homestretch in that race, and the other horses look like little specks in the far distance. Secretariat, like Seabiscuit, was a horse who had gotten "in touch" with the purpose for which he was made, and the results were spectacular.

Thirty-one lengths. What do we know about a horse that wins a race by thirty-one lengths? One thing we know about him: he isn't racing in order to compare himself to other horses. If all he wanted was to beat the second-best horse, wouldn't a victory by two lengths or five suffice? Maybe ten if he wanted to rub it in a little. But a horse who wins by thirty-one lengths has forgotten about all the other horses. He's running from some other motivation besides mere competition.

If your daughter's idea of character is based on comparison with the girls around her, she's not going to be a girl of especially strong character. If her goal is to be a little more moral or a little more honest or a little kinder than the next girl, she's not going to be very moral or very honest or very kind. A person of character lives out God's plan for her life without regard to what anybody else around her is doing.

Character isn't a competition. Character is the joy of running the race set before you and feeling God's pleasure as a result.

DON'T FORGET: Raising our daughters to become the women God meant for them to be is our sole purpose!

Chapter 6

Empowerment

 One of our great success stories at Big Oak Ranch is Jessica. She was fifteen when she came to us, and she couldn't read or write. She had never been to school a day in her life. Supposedly she had been homeschooled, but her mother never educated her.

I always sit down with every new child at the Ranch and ask them about their goals. Jessica's goal, she said, was to graduate on time. Fifteen years old and couldn't read or write, but she wanted to graduate with the other kids her age. I took a deep breath. "All right," I said. "It's going to take some hard work. I can't do this for you. It's up to you."

To see Jessica on her first day of ninth grade, you would have never known she had never been to school before.

She took to it like a duck to water. Academically, there was plenty of catching up to do. But she was determined. She put in the work and showed tremendous progress. The more her teachers and Ranch family believed in her, the more she believed in herself. She was elected class representative that ninth-grade year, and in the years after that. When she was a senior, she was the class chaplain.

Jessica did graduate with the rest of her class. Four years later, she had a college degree. Shortly after Jessica graduated from Auburn University, I went by the offices of the radio personalities Rick and Bubba and put in a good word for Jessica. She's a powerhouse, I told them. She'd make a great intern for your show.

I talked to Jessica a week or so later. I was going to tell her that I had talked to Rick and Bubba on her behalf and that she should get in touch with them, but before I got around to mentioning it she said, "Oh, I went by and spoke with Rick and Bubba the other day."

"Spoke with Rick and Bubba?" I said. "How'd you do that?"

"I just knocked on their door. They let me in, and I asked them for a job. We had been talking for a while, and they said, 'Oh, now we know who you are. John Croyle told us about you.'"

"Wait," I said. "You didn't lead with that? You didn't tell them you knew me? That you lived at Big Oak?"

"I didn't see that it mattered," she said.

Jessica had marched right up to the door of two of the most well-known radio personalities in the country, knocked on the door, and introduced herself with (as far as she knew) no prior introduction. She didn't drop any names, didn't play the "Big Oak card" (though I have told her over and over that she ought to play that card anytime she thinks it will help).

Speaking of Jessica's reluctance to play the "Big Oak card," for a couple of years at Auburn, Jessica worked for Mike Hubbard and his wife. Mike is the Auburn Football Network Leader and Speaker of the House of Representatives in Montgomery, Alabama. I called Mike to ask if I could talk to him about Jessica for a short documentary we were making. He seemed genuinely surprised. "Why would you want to talk to me about Jessica?" he asked. In the two years of working for Mike and his wife, Jessica had never mentioned that she had lived at the Ranch. She wasn't interested in getting any special treatment.

When Jessica graduated from Auburn, I told her, "A lot of people who have had everything handed to them are going to compete with you for a job someday. And they're going to lose." I would put Jessica up against anybody I've met before in my life.

One year after graduation, Jessica worked for ESPN. That's a long way from someone who couldn't read or write at fifteen years old.

Jessica's story is a story of empowerment. When she came to us, nobody had ever shown her that they believed in her. As her teachers and houseparents told her that she had what it takes, she began to believe it. Here's one of the big things I have learned from Jessica: a girl who feels empowered is a girl who is free from fear.

> A girl who feels empowered is a girl who is free from fear.

On a side note: Jessica's younger sister, Michelle, came to the Ranch at the same time Jessica did with the same obstacles ahead of her. Michelle is now a junior at the University of Alabama in the School of Nursing. Yes, encouragement will lead to empowerment.

The Proverbs 31 Woman

The Excellent Woman of Proverbs 31 is a woman who feels empowered. In chapter 3 we saw the ways she shows initiative. That is a kind of empowerment. In verse 11, we see one of the fruits of her empowerment: "The heart of her husband safely trusts her; so he will have no lack of gain"

(NKJV). Her husband trusts in her competence. Do you think he could trust her so completely if she weren't empowered and confident?

This is a strong woman we're talking about here. But notice that her strength is not something she exerts for her own gain. An Excellent Woman, when she is empowered, uses that power to benefit others. Her husband has no lack of gain. She provides food for her household, including her maidservants (v. 15). She reaches out to the poor (v. 20). And ultimately, her children rise up and call her blessed. There are women (just as there are men) who use power to lord it over others. But that's not the use to which the Excellent Woman puts her power.

"Strength and honor are her clothing," according to verse 25; "She shall rejoice in time to come" (NKJV). There it is again: the woman clothed in strength is a woman who has no fear. She doesn't dread the future, but instead rejoices at the thought of what lies ahead for her.

When one of our girls, and yours too, leaves us to go out on their own after high school, whether they are going to college, vocational school, the armed forces, etc., they *all* have this look of excitement and uncertainty. Some have extreme confidence and others have severe concerns, and ask themselves, "Can I do this?"

Show me a young lady "clothed in strength and honor" and I'll show you a girl whose parents gave her a sense of empowerment. She is fearless like Jessica during her job search and interviews.

Strength, especially strength founded in the Lord, *will* remove fear. Courage is simply the correct handling of your fear. The Proverbs 31 Woman, and hopefully your daughter and ours, have a truckload of fearlessness grounded in wise counsel they received from you and me as their parents and preparers. They have empowerment that comes solely from knowing that God is going to get them through whatever obstacles come their way.

> *They have empowerment that comes solely from knowing that God is going to get them through whatever obstacles come their way.*

Insecure Arrogance vs. Humble Confidence

For the Proverbs 31 Woman, empowerment means, among other things, being empowered to serve others. It's not all about self. There is a huge connection between godly empowerment and humility. Arrogance is a sure sign of insecurity. Humility, on the other hand, is a real source of real power in itself.

Many years ago when I was a counselor at a summer camp in Mississippi (the same camp where the vision of Big Oak Ranch was born), I got a close look at the difference between insecure arrogance and humble power. The electricity went out at the camp, which is a serious enough problem in itself. But we had an additional problem on top of it: our water for the camp relied on electric pumps. So no electricity meant no water either. Scrambling for a plan, we decided to take the campers to a nearby state park and pitch tents. We had a problem though; we didn't have enough tents for all the campers. The camp owner sent me and another counselor to a nearby army installation (Camp Shelby) to see if they would let us borrow a few tents.

We asked around the installation to find out who we should ask about borrowing some tents, and we were directed to a second lieutenant, a little bantam rooster of a man whose Napoleonic complex seemed to be exaggerated by his relatively low rank. When we asked about the tents, he didn't just tell us no. He threw in a first-rate cussing for free. There was no mistaking it: this man loved the opportunity to use his power to refuse our simple request.

The second lieutenant sent us packing. We stood beside our car trying to figure out what to do next, and the longer we stood there, the madder I got about being treated that way. I decided to go over the second lieutenant's head.

We found the general of Camp Shelby at his house watering his flowers. We got out of the car and introduced ourselves. I explained who we were, where we had come from, and what we needed. The general was gracious, kind, and very happy to help. "Sure," he said, "we have plenty of tents around here. You're welcome to as many as you need. Just let me make one phone call."

Who do you think he called? You guessed it. He called the second lieutenant who had cussed us and sent us away empty-handed. He didn't seem all that happy to see us when he drove up to the general's house. The general said, "Give these boys anything they need!" The lieutenant then gave us the tents we needed.

Arrogance always has its Waterloo. People delight to see the arrogant get their come-uppance. To put it another way, you can either be humble, or you can be humiliated. Humility is the most powerful tool you can use for power. In the world's eyes, that's a paradox. The world views power in terms of the ability to get your own way; they feel that power is aggressiveness.

Real Power: The Power to Make a Difference

Real power is the power to choose and accomplish that which you know to be best. Powerlessness is the feeling that all the choices are being made for you. A powerless person feels that she cannot make a difference in her own life or in anybody else's.

One girl who came to the Ranch told me a story of what the life she came from was like. This illustrates what powerlessness feels like. When she sat in her den, reading or watching television, her mother would sometimes come by and smack her upside the head—hard enough to knock her into the floor. As the tears welled in her eyes, the girl would ask her mother, "What did I do?"

"Nothing," her mother would say.

"Then why did you hit me?"

"Because I could."

That is a terribly skewed view of power. Because she had "power" over her little girl, that woman thought she had the right to abuse her if she chose. No doubt this woman felt powerless in other areas of her life. But randomly hitting her daughter was only the tip of the iceberg. This same woman was prostituting her daughter to various men for ten dollars a pop from the time the little girl was four or five until we got her at age twelve.

Most of us can't imagine the powerlessness that this girl felt, but I can tell you it was soul-crushing. In our first interview I looked at her and said, "You don't trust anybody, do you?"

She answered with a question: "Why would I?"

"I promise you there will be a day when you will trust me," I assured her.

She learned to trust. She will literally come running down the hall to give me a hug and tell me she loves me. I tell her the same. She's going to be a *great* woman one day because she is realizing she is *not* under an abusive parent's power anymore. How liberating is that feeling! Look into her eyes, and you'll see "it"! She has that humble confidence that comes from believing in yourself.

We recognized the good in her and pointed out what she was good at. Her trust gave her a sense of empowerment. Or maybe her sense of empowerment made it possible for her to trust. It's not always easy to see which comes first in a situation like that. In any case, when a new girl comes to the Ranch now, she's the first to go up to her and reassure her that she has come to a good place.

Power can come from position, or power can come from personality. Any fool can exercise power if he gets himself into a position that carries authority. The second lieutenant I mentioned earlier had power that came from his position. This kind of power is usually short-lived. But then there are people whose power comes from their personality, their character, their sense of knowing right and wrong, and believing in themselves to stand up for what they *know* is right! This is the kind of power we want our girls to have. This power will carry them into eternity.

Practical Helps and Suggestions

So how do you teach your daughter to be empowered? Remember, your goal here is not only to help her walk on her own but to help others first. Here are some practical tips for instilling empowerment in your daughter.

Help your daughter know who she is—including her limits.

In the previous chapter we talked about character as becoming who you were made to be. There's a lot of power in being who you were made to be. We talked about "living in your sweet spot." That in itself is a kind of empowerment. Help your daughter know exactly who she is. That includes helping her know her limitations.

A Clydesdale will never outrun a Thoroughbred. It just isn't going to happen. But that's okay, because a thoroughbred will never out-pull a Clydesdale. As long as each horse understands what it was made for, and lives out of that understanding, things will go well for them both. Imagine if a Clydesdale devoted its life to racing or a Thoroughbred tried to make a career at the pulling competitions at county fairs. Both horses would feel as if they were severely lacking in power simply because they were choosing or being placed in a position they were *not* meant to be in.

When we try to live vicariously through our children, either reliving glory days or trying to live down old failures, we deny them the power of living out the exact lives that God made them to live and meant for them to experience.

Teach your daughter to pray.

When we live by our own power, we're never going to be any more powerful or effective than the upper limits of our own power and effectiveness. Perhaps I'm stating the obvious here. But when we open ourselves up to the power of God—our heavenly Father who only wants the best for us—then suddenly there are *no* limits. That's what happens when we teach our daughters to pray and trust God for the results.

> *Help your daughter know exactly who she is. That includes helping her know her limitations.*

How do you teach your daughters to pray? By praying with them. Prayer is yet another thing that is best taught by example. Your daughters need to see you pray. Let me emphasize here that I don't mean some cute little bedtime nursery rhyme that has been memorized. I mean real, honest, and specific prayers. It can be extremely helpful to keep a prayer chart or journal that you share with your daughter. Record what you prayed, when you prayed for it, and then how that prayer was answered and when.

Having let her see and hear you praying, let her also see the divine results of those prayers.

Give your daughter opportunities to trust God.

I have a writer friend who found himself one day in a very tough spot financially. He had no idea how he was going to buy groceries for the week or pay the mortgage for the month. He and his wife discussed the situation, looking for solutions, but they came up short.

The family was eating a lunch put together from the last leftovers in the refrigerator when they heard the familiar sound of the mailman's truck. There was a joke in the house that the four-year-old Brittany was the "Check Girl." She had a reputation for bringing in checks when she got the mail; her siblings mostly brought back bills. That was the story, anyway. So my friend turned to little Brittany and said, "All right, Check Girl. It's up to you. Go out to the mailbox and bring us back a check."

Eager to help, Brittany jumped off her stool and headed down the driveway. Meanwhile, my friend's wife was staring daggers at him. "You shouldn't put Brittany in that position," she said. "It's not fair to her." He shrugged. He was just joking with his little girl, but he realized that his wife was probably right; it wasn't right to put that kind of pressure on Brittany.

But when Brittany got back from the mailbox, she had in her hand a couple of bills, a few pieces of junk mail, and a royalty check for two thousand dollars. Bear in mind, my friend had never received a two-thousand-dollar royalty check in his life. He hasn't received one since. This was a one-time special situation, as if God were winking at him, showing him that the faith of a little girl was more powerful than the doubts and fears of her two parents.

Trust God yourself if you want your daughter to trust God.

How can you help give your daughter opportunities to trust God? One thing you can know for sure: you can't do it by playing it too safe. You have to step out in faith. Trust God yourself if you want your daughter to trust God. Remember children listen with their eyes. What they see you do will far outweigh anything you say.

Teach your daughter to steward the power of the tongue.

One characteristic of a powerful person is that people take her words seriously. There's a man on our Board of Directors at Big Oak Ranch named Jim Leonard. He hardly ever says anything. But every time he speaks, everybody leans in to hear what he has to say. He's like the E. F. Hutton of the Board. We know that his words matter and they carry weight and merit.

It is extremely important that your daughter not scatter or dilute the power of her tongue by talking too much, or not talking to the point. Nobody ever killed an elephant with a shotgun. But even a small rifle, if you hit the right spot, can bring the biggest elephant down.

Girls have a tendency to chatter away; that's just how God made them. I don't suggest that you should try to turn your daughter into Jim Leonard. But you do need to teach your daughter not to use her words for slander or gossip, not to lie, and not to let talk become frivolous or coarse. She wants people to take her seriously.

Steer your daughter away from false modes of power.

People who feel that they don't have any real power have a tendency to find other ways they can feel powerful. For today's girls, there are two main (and related) ways that they do this: online media and old-fashioned girl drama.

Thanks to social media, for the first time in history, girls are able to quantify their popularity in measurable numbers. She puts a picture or a comment or a video on a social media site. Then she waits for people to "like" or "favorite" her picture or comment or video. Kids spend much of their time staring at their cell phones, waiting for those "likes" and "favorites" to roll in.

It's amazing how much of a teenager's self-worth is tied up in how many people respond to her on social media. You remember what it was like when you were in junior high and high school; people were obsessed with their social status. Can you imagine how bad the obsession would have been if you had been able to put a number on it? That's the world your kids live in. Social media has some great uses, but it also presents a false mode of power. One of the best ways to break its hold on your daughter is to ensure that she feels that she has actual power in the world and not just virtual power.

The second mode of false power I want to mention is "girl drama." You remember the little dramas of middle school and high school, in which the popular girls lord it over the less popular girls. We discussed this in the "Righteousness" chapter. Girls like to get into each other's business and vie for "Queen Bee" status. It's all false power. Proverbs has this to say about "girl drama": "Like one who takes a dog by the ears is he who passes by and meddles with strife not belonging to him" (26:17 NASB). Urge your daughter to excuse herself from the drama.

A powerful person is confident and satisfied (but still hungry).

We have a young girl who is a really good athlete, and she's aspiring to go to a college to compete with other "like-minded" athletes at that level. She recently competed in the State Championship in her event, and she won. When I saw her afterward, she was beaming from ear to ear.

I asked her, "What now?"

She replied, "Next year, the State record!" She was confident and satisfied, yet she was already looking ahead and knew that there was more for her to do.

Her childhood was *not* one to smile about, and she received *no* encouragement to succeed prior to coming to the Ranch. Yet with the positive reenforcement that she received from her houseparents and coaches, she was able to shrug off the uncertainty she had before and blossom into one of the most gifted runners I have ever seen.

> *Great parenting never settles when there is another level to achieve and the child has the ability and drive to get there.*

Great parenting *never* settles when there is another level to achieve and the child has the ability and drive to get there. Celebrate their victory with them, and then help them in pressing forward to the next goal.

A powerful person gets tired, but never exhausted.

My wife is a calculus teacher, and she's truly one of the smartest people I know. I have seen her grade test paper after test paper and be so very tired, but she still puts together an awesome lesson plan for the next day.

I will sometimes look at one of her problems she is teaching her students how to solve, and I am exhausted just listening how to solve it, much less trying to solve it myself. It looks like a different language!

On the flip side, I have had speaking engagements in front of five thousand people and it's *not* an issue for me. I've long since gotten over those butterflies that sometimes come with public speaking. But do I sometimes get tired? Sure.

Ask Tee to speak, and I see her tighten up. She speaks in front of her classroom but does not do speaking engagements. She has told me before it would be exhausting to do what I do.

The point is, we are both doing what we were built and formed to do. Fish swim, horses run, and your daughter has this power within her. If she is doing what she was meant to do and using her God-given talents, she might get tired but never exhausted.

Conclusion

I am a huge Mother Teresa fan. She was a woman of tremendous power, and not one drop of that power came from
her position. It was all about her character and personality.
In 1984, Mother Teresa's order of nuns, the Missionaries
of Charity, went to a convent in Norristown, Pennsylvania,
a suburb of Philadelphia. Their goal was to build a soup
kitchen and a shelter to serve the homeless in the area. The
locals weren't too sure about that plan. They wanted the
homeless out of their neighborhood; they didn't want to
invite them in with free food and shelter! And technically
speaking, they had a legal leg to stand on. The neighborhood
where the nuns wanted to build the shelter was zoned for
single-family houses and office space. It appeared that they
were going to be able to keep the shelter out.

While the fight was ongoing, Mother Teresa came
to town to visit the nuns in this newest outpost of the
Missionaries of Charity. She attended Mass one Sunday
morning, and afterwards she asked to meet with the borough council members and business owners who opposed
the shelter. They agreed to the meeting.

Once everybody was in the room, Mother Teresa opened
in prayer. When she began to speak on behalf of the poorest
people in Norristown, she spoke softly, barely above a whis-
per, according to one of the men who was there. By the time
the meeting was over, everybody in the room had given up

their opposition to the project. Their various official positions were no match for the power and authority that a little old lady brought to the table.

Sam Vallone, a borough council member, later said, "I've met two presidents, and I was awed by the significance of their office. Then here comes this little old lady who had no office, but has done so much for humanity." When the meeting was over, Vallone said what everybody else on the council must have been thinking: "I want to make it clear that Sam Vallone will not go on record as voting against a saint."

That's the kind of power we want our girls to exercise.

Chapter 7

Servant-Heartedness

 I started writing this chapter in a Chick-fil-A. If you have ever been to a Chick-fil-A restaurant, you probably know how appropriate it is to write about servant-heartedness in one. The chain is legendary for customer service. When you come in the door, there's a sign that says, "It is our pleasure to serve you." When you ask the person behind the counter for anything, his or her response will almost certainly be, "It will be my pleasure."

The employees of Chick-fil-A are always friendly, helpful, clean-cut—and when they say it's their pleasure to serve, you actually believe them. By all appearances, they actually *do* find pleasure in serving others. That culture of service comes straight from Truett Cathy, the founder of

Chick-fil-A and one of the most renowned servant-leaders in corporate America. There are all sorts of stories to be told about this down-to-earth leader's willingness to serve others. One of the most telling is the fact that every Sunday (all Chick-fil-A restaurants are closed on Sunday, by the way), Truett Cathy is at church teaching the Sunday school class he's been teaching for fifty years. Think about that: the multi-millionaire founder of one of the most successful fast-food chains in America takes time out of his busy schedule every week to serve his fellow church-goers by teaching a Sunday school class.

It's pretty impressive how the culture of servant-heartedness trickles down from the Cathy family to the employees of Chick-fil-A. But here's something even more impressive: the culture of servant-heartedness trickles down even further, to the customers! Next time you're in a Chick-fil-A, look around. I suspect you'll notice that it's a good bit cleaner than most other fast-food restaurants.

Why?

One reason, the obvious reason, is that Chick-fil-A's employees are unusually efficient and unusually committed to keeping their restaurant clean. But there's another, less obvious reason: customers who eat at Chick-fil-A are more likely to clean up after themselves rather than leaving a mess for somebody else to clean up. I don't have statistics to back this up; I'm just telling what I've observed. At other fast-food restaurants I see people get up and leave their table piled with wrappers and French fry boxes; I don't see many Chick-fil-A customers do that. In the three hours I sat working on this book, I saw four different customers wipe up the crumbs and ketchup stains before they left their table. Never mind that the highly efficient and capable Chick-fil-A employee would be coming right behind to clean up.

Why would they do that? I think it's because the people at Chick-fil-A make it obvious that serving others truly can be a pleasure. They give customers respect, and their customers give them respect right back. When I go to Chick-fil-A, I'm reminded that servant-heartedness isn't a one-way street. A person who takes pleasure in serving others is a person who inspires others to serve as well. When we teach our daughters to be servant-hearted, we aren't teaching them to be doormats or martyrs (we'll return to martyrs a little later). Doormats and martyrs don't inspire servant-heartedness in other people; but real servant-heartedness inspires others to serve. It seems strange, but by modeling servant-heartedness for your daughter, you won't only be teaching her

> *A person who takes pleasure in serving others is a person who inspires others to serve as well.*

to serve; you may also put her in a position to *be* served by those who surround her.

By nature, people seek to be served. Children come out of the womb expecting others to meet their needs (perfectly understandable, considering the fact that they *can't* meet their own needs), but unless they are trained differently, they continue in that path, looking to be served rather than to serve. Unless they are trained differently, people tend to assume that it is better to receive than to give, to be served rather than to serve.

You've been to those dinner parties where the men head into the next room after the meal to talk while the women clean up the kitchen. The women serve while the men take it easy. My dad taught me a secret a long time ago: it's more fun in the kitchen. It was his habit to wash dishes with the women after supper was over. There was a ripple effect—I now do the same thing at parties. I don't expect you to congratulate me for helping out in the kitchen. I do it because I want to do it, and I saw it modeled before me my whole life.

One day a friend of mine told me, "You changed my husband's life!" I was a little surprised to hear it. I didn't remember having any life-changing conversation with this woman's husband. "You washed dishes in our kitchen after a party," the woman said, "and it changed my husband's life. Now, when we go to a party, he always helps the women in the kitchen rather than sitting out in the living room with the men."

A very wealthy man told me of a hunting trip he went on with our son Brodie. After dinner, Brodie got up and cleared the table and went to the kitchen to help. His act of service impressed this man.

All of us have discovered that servant-heartedness isn't a chore, but a pleasure. And the ripple effect can be traced back to my dad. That's the kind of contagious service that we can expect when we raise our children in an environment where people are able to say, "It's my pleasure to serve you" in their words and in their actions.

The Servant Heart of the Proverbs 31 Woman

We previously discussed the nurturing spirit of the Excellent Woman of Proverbs 31. There is certainly overlap between nurture and servant-heartedness. The main difference in my use of the two terms is that nurture is about taking care of the people who "belong" to you (that is, family), and servant-heartedness is about taking care of people outside the family. Some of the same habits apply, of course. It's the difference between inreach and outreach.

The Proverbs 31 Woman looked to her family first. But there was something left over for people outside her family. "She extends her hand to the poor, and she stretches out her hands to the needy" (v. 20 NASB). To put the verse in context, this discussion of the Excellent Woman's charitable spirit comes right after the discussion of her hard work and her business sense. Everything this woman does is *other-centered*. In verse 19 she reaches her hand out to the distaff (which is part of a loom for making fabric), then she reaches out her hand to the poor. It's an interesting parallel. Her hard work isn't just for personal gain, but also for the benefit of the less fortunate. That's a servant's heart in action.

Going the Extra Mile

The idea of "going the extra mile" is so common—especially in a customer service context (there's that word "service" again)—that it's easy to forget where the term originated. It was Jesus who came up with the idea of going the extra mile. He said, "Whoever forces you to go one mile, go with him two" (Matt. 5:41 NASB).

A little context will help here. In Jesus' time, when the Romans ruled Israel, Roman law stated that any Roman soldier traveling on the road could require a Jew to carry his pack for a mile. He didn't have the right to force the Jew to carry his pack for any more than one mile, but the Jew couldn't refuse to carry the pack for a mile or less. As you can imagine, this didn't sit well with the Jews. They found it humiliating to be forced to serve their oppressors in that way.

Jesus' listeners at the Sermon on the Mount must have been shocked, then, when he said, "Whoever forces you to go one mile, go with him two." They must have thought he was a glutton for punishment. In fact, this is a brilliant picture of what it means to have a servant heart. Jesus was saying, in effect, "The Romans can force you to carry their pack one mile. But nobody can force you to take it two." That forced mile might have been a sign of oppression, but the second mile was a sign of freedom. The extra mile is something that a person does of his own free will.

The point I'm trying to make is that being a servant is a very different thing from being a slave. A person with a servant heart is a person who has vision and initiative, who takes charge of a situation. This is such an important distinction. In raising a daughter with a servant heart, you're not raising somebody to be ordered around. You're raising

> *You're raising somebody who acts out of her own understanding that living for others is more fulfilling than living for self.*

somebody who acts out of her own understanding that living for others is more fulfilling than living for self.

In telling his listeners to carry a Roman soldier's pack a second mile, Jesus was telling them to be proactive, to take charge through service. He was telling them to be servant leaders. And, of course, nobody has ever displayed servant leadership like Jesus. While the disciples were jockeying for position and arguing about who was going to get the honor of being the greatest in Jesus' kingdom, Jesus knelt down and started washing their feet—the lowliest job assigned to the lowliest servant in a household. The first will be last, he reminded them, and the last will be first. That's not just religious talk. It's true. Everybody wants their kids to end up on top. Why do you think parents spend so many billions of dollars every year on SAT and ACT tutors and personal coaches and violin lessons? But if you're really serious about making sure your daughter finishes first, and if you take Jesus at his word, it might be time to give her some lessons in servanthood. The rewards to these lessons are *priceless.*

Martyrs versus Servants

We all admire martyrs. I mean real martyrs, the people who actually die for their faith, choosing to sacrifice their lives rather than deny Christ. Unfortunately, there are a lot of people in the world who seek out a kind of false martyrdom that gives real martyrs a bad name. You've known people like this. They seem to think that their calling in life is to suffer by being a doormat for people who mistreat them and take advantage of them. And equally unfortunately, there are a lot of people who equate that kind of false martyrdom with servant-heartedness.

So I'd like to set the record straight. Servanthood and martyrdom, whether true martyrdom or false martyrdom, are very different things. We want to encourage a servant's heart in our daughters. We want to discourage false martyrdom.

As I said, people admire genuine martyrs. The problem is you don't know any genuine martyrs. By definition, a genuine martyr is dead; his or her death—the voluntary giving up of life—is evidence of true martyrdom. The problem with false martyrdom is that a person is trying, through "self-sacrifice," to get the kind of admiration that we reserve for people who make the ultimate sacrifice. The great irony of false martyrdom is that it's a way of using "self-sacrifice" as a means of inflating the self.

So, in the interest of clarity, here is a chart illustrating the difference between a servant's heart and a martyr complex:

A True Servant	A False Martyr
Looks for ways to meet other people's needs.	Tends to other people's needs as a way of building up his or her own self.
Doesn't care whether he or she is recognized or not.	Needs to be seen and recognized, even though that need is usually cloaked in false humility.
Leads by example.	Doesn't lead (because no one wants to follow a martyr's example).
Makes people want to be like him or her.	Is unattractive—turns people off.
Inspires other people to step up and serve.	Gets dumped on. Inspires the attitude, "Well, if this person wants to clean up my messes, I'm happy to leave more messes."

To sum it up, a false martyr needs for his or her acts of service to be seen, but a true servant doesn't care who sees. A true servant knows that God sees. I do think that people see and recognize a servant. But that's not the motivation for a true servant. And a true servant certainly doesn't feel the need to get recognition for every act of service.

Wet Beds and Servant Hearts

A friend of mine told me about a summer camp where he worked that nicely illustrates what I mean by a servant heart as opposed to a martyr complex. Like a lot of summer camps, this camp was staffed by college-aged counselors— college-aged boys, since this was a boys' camp. Now, college-aged boys aren't exactly known for their ability to put other people's needs ahead of their own. But this was a pretty special group of guys, and well-trained to boot.

There was a kid at the camp who wet his bed every night of the month. Then he came back the next year and wet his bed every night again. And the next year. And the next year. We're talking about more than a hundred nights of wet beds over the course of this kid's camp career. Every morning, when the boys left their cabins to go to their morning worship service, one of his counselors would go back to the cabin, strip the wet sheets from his bed, put on new, identical sheets, and run the wet sheets down to the laundry. Every single morning, the counselors handled that boy's urine. For more than a hundred mornings.

Oh and here's the other thing: this kid was awful. He was mean to the other campers, disrespectful to the counselors, ungrateful for what they did for him. But here's the most incredible thing of all. After all of that—four years of month-long camp terms—none of that boy's cabin mates ever knew that he was a bed-wetter. The counselors never failed to change his sheets. They never let a hint or a comment slip that might tip off the other boys that there was a bed-wetter in their midst, though they surely felt from time to time that a little humiliation would do the mean, ungrateful little brat some good. No, they were so committed to protecting that little boy's dignity that they never let themselves even drop the slightest hint about the distasteful job they had to do for him every single day. They were servants, not martyrs. They didn't need any particular credit for the ways they served their camper.

But God saw what they were up to.

Respecting those who serve for a living.

Your daughter is going to learn a lot about the value of service from watching the way you deal with people in the various service industries. How do you treat servers in restaurants or the housekeeping staff at a hotel or the overworked but frustratingly inefficient woman behind the counter at the Department of Motor Vehicles? I'm not equating the "service sector" with the kind of servant-heartedness that we're talking about in this chapter. But I do think this is a relevant issue. If your daughter sees you speak rudely or disparagingly to the man behind the counter at the dry cleaners, if she sees you getting frustrated at the yard man because English isn't his first language and he's not sure what you're trying to tell him, you're communicating that you value power more than you value people. A servant heart finds it very hard to grow in that environment.

When I was twenty-three and still immature and pretty stupid, I found myself on an elevator with Bill Bright, the founder of Campus Crusade for Christ. This was one of those old-fashioned elevators that still had a man operating it—which gives you some idea of how long it has been since I was twenty-three! We were at a conference, and Bill Bright was one of the keynote speakers. In other words, it was a very busy couple of days for him. As far as doing his duty to spread the gospel, he was going to more than meet his quota with his keynote speech to several thousand people. If Bill Bright wanted to take the day off from evangelizing, nobody would blame him. But during the two or three minutes we were on that elevator, Bill Bright was talking the whole time to the operator; eye-to-eye, man-to-man, as if that young man was the only other person in the world. He asked about the elevator operator's eternal soul, and though the young man didn't receive Christ on the spot, Mr. Bright gave him quite a bit to think about.

That made a huge impression on me. Still pretty self-absorbed at twenty-three, it didn't occur to me to say one thing to that elevator operator except, "Ground Floor." But Bill Bright had the heart of a servant. He was always thinking about what the people around him needed. And the elevator operator needed the Lord.

Many of our children start their careers in food service. I have heard from them that the most dreaded shift for many restaurant workers is the Sunday lunch shift. That's when the churchgoers come in. And people fresh from church have a terrible reputation for rudeness and for being poor tippers. What do we communicate to our children about the value of service when we treat servers that way? It's a far cry from what I saw in Bill Bright that day.

Practical Helps and Suggestions

Children, as I have already mentioned, are born self-ish. Servant-heartedness is not something your daughter is likely to pick up on her own. She has to be trained in it. Or, perhaps more accurately, she has to catch it from you. Here are some practical ways to grow a servant's heart in your daughter.

From Initiation to Initiative.

It is important for your daughter to have opportuni-ties to practice servant-heartedness from the very earliest age. Little children like to help their parents. Take advan-tage of that natural tendency and nurture it; keep an eye out for age-appropriate ways your daughter can help. Your three-year-old can't fold a load of laundry, but she can help sort socks. She can't scrub the pots and pans after supper, but she may be able to dry the plastic containers. This is *initiation*. Your daughter is being introduced to the rhythms of service and being allowed to participate in low-stakes ways.

Take advantage of that natural tendency and nurture it; keep an eye out for age-appropriate ways your daughter can help.

One thing I should mention about initiation: it will almost always be easier just to do the work yourself rather than allowing a toddler into your domain and handing over tasks that you could do ten times faster and better. Resist the temptation to send your daughter off to watch television or play with her dolls while you just knock out the work by yourself. The point of initiation isn't to get the work done efficiently, but to get your daughter involved. The parent-daughter conversations you have while you're folding clothes and she's sorting socks are one of the key ways that your daughter will come to understand that it truly is a pleasure to serve others. Remember, you're painting a picture for your daughter: servant-heartedness is a good, rewarding way to live.

As your daughter gets older, initiation turns to *training*. "Would you sort these socks with me?" becomes "Could you divide the laundry into lights and darks," which becomes

"Please fold this load with me," which becomes "Please be in charge of laundry today." You're still looking for age-appropriate tasks, but what you will find is that if you start your child early in the habits of service, she can do more than you might expect of a person her age. Always say please and thank you, and guess what, they will "catch" these manners essential to real life.

A key part of training is to praise your daughter when she shows initiative. Keep the end in mind: you want her to know that serving others is a pleasure. Praise her for a heart of service, not just the results of her work. Having said that, however, let me offer this qualifier: your daughter might as well do things right when she does them. In other words, praise her for her willingness to serve, but still train her in the proper ways of doing the work. How many well-meant Mother's Day "breakfasts in bed" have resulted in mothers having extra work cleaning up the mess made by her sweet children? It's okay for you to say, "Breakfast in bed! What a surprise! While I enjoy this (burnt) toast, will you go make sure the kitchen is put back in order?"

The end result of initiation and training will be *initiative*. The day will come when you will say, "Can you help with laundry today?" and your daughter will answer, "I've already done it." That's your goal—not only because it lightens your load when your children help with the housework, but, more important, because you have succeeded in convincing your daughter that it is better to serve than to be served.

Make sure the girls and women in your family are served as well as serving.

I vividly remember the time my grandmother got the flu. She lay in bed, hardly able to move for days. It was scary to me because my grandmother was always bustling around taking care of everybody, and here she was unable even to sit up straight. But what I remember most about that time was when my grandfather came in with the biscuit bowl. He also brought the flour, shortening, and buttermilk that my grandmother used for mixing up biscuits. He brought the bowl to my grandmother's bedside so she could pour the correct amount of each item into the biscuit bowl. With a groan and a great effort she rolled onto her side and reached her hand into the bowl and kneaded the flour, shortening, and buttermilk into biscuit dough by muscle memory. She never even opened her eyes.

My grandfather was a good man with more than his share of good qualities. But that wasn't his greatest moment as a husband or as an example to his grandson. That would have been an excellent opportunity to serve his sick wife. He could have brought a meal to his wife's bedside—a sandwich maybe, or maybe some biscuits that represented his best effort at cooking, even if they turned out terrible. Instead, it seems his thought pattern was, "I want some biscuits. My biscuit maker is sick in bed. I'll bring the biscuit bowl to her so she can take care of me without even getting out of bed."

If you are a father, your daughter needs to see you serving your wife. She needs to see you serving alongside your wife. You don't want your daughter to have the idea that women are pack mules, drudging away in the service of their menfolk. She needs to know that servant-heartedness is a mutual thing among people who love one another. I keep saying that you want to create an environment where people can truthfully say, "It is my pleasure to serve you." Dad, you have the power to send that message ten times more powerfully than your wife can. When your daughter sees her mother serving cheerfully, that's going to make an impression on her. When she sees her mother's cheerful service answered with her father's service back to her, that's huge. She begins to understand that serving others doesn't drain

> *Serving others doesn't drain away the self, but is a source of replenishment and builds strength of character.*

away the self, but is a source of replenishment and builds strength of character.

Pull, don't push.

We all want our daughters to have the heart of a servant. But there is a danger in pushing your daughter too hard toward service. You don't want to build resentment. Rather than pushing your daughter to serve, think of yourself as pulling her along. Invite her to join in as you serve. Take her with you to a nursing home or soup kitchen to *watch* you work with those people who need help. Before you know it, she will be right beside you helping with a servant-hearted joy.

Don't reward self-sacrifice in ways that steal the joy of self-sacrifice.

I want to say a short word about the way we parents reward our children when they show initiative in serving others. It is vitally important that you notice and offer praise when your daughter demonstrates a servant's heart. Nothing gives a parent as much joy as when his or her child shows real character and a willingness to sacrifice for the sake of others. When your daughter shares her ice cream with the friend who's crying because she dropped her own, you want to run right up to the counter and buy her a double-scoop cone to replace the one she gave away.

I'd just like to point out that the real reward for servant-heartedness is the joy of knowing that you have done the right thing. When you praise your daughter for her acts of kindness and service, start here. "Hey baby, I sure am proud of the way you gave away your ice cream to Camille. That was sweet!" If you exuberantly go get your daughter a double as a reward for giving her ice cream away, you take away some of the natural, built-in reward that God put into the act of sacrifice. Sure, a double ice cream is a pleasure, but you need to let your daughter feel the full pleasure that comes from giving of herself. She needs to know that self-sacrifice can give even more pleasure than ice cream. I don't mean that you should never give your daughter a treat as a reward for serving others. I'm just saying that you don't want to send the message that servant-heartedness is just another way to get more treats.

Put your daughter's acts of service into context.

There's an old story about a man who walked past a group of three brick masons on a construction site for a new cathedral. He asked the first brick mason, "What are you doing?" The brick mason said, "What does it look like I'm doing? I'm laying brick." The man asked the second brick mason, "What are you doing?" The second brick mason answered, "I'm building a wall." The man asked the third brick mason, "What are you doing?" The third brick mason answered, "I'm building a beautiful cathedral where people will come to worship and God will be glorified. Hymns of praise will echo in these walls, and the village poor will come here when they need help, and young men will bring young women here to marry and start their new lives together, and from miles around people will be able to see the steeple of this cathedral and know that God loves us and lives among us."

Children aren't always good at seeing the big picture. If your daughter sees acts of service in the short-sighted way of the first brick mason or even the second brick mason, she is going to find it hard to keep it up. One of the best things you can do for her is to help her see the big picture. She's not just serving others. She's building the kingdom of God.

> *She's not just serving others. She's building the kingdom of God.*

Conclusion

We have a tradition at Big Oak Ranch that has become a key part of our Christmas season. Every year, each house family "adopts" a needy family in the area and buys presents for them. The Ranch kids pool their money and decide what the kids in their "adopted" family might like and they go shopping for them.

The beginning of that tradition is one of my favorite stories from our years at the Ranch. One of our houseparents found out about a family that wasn't even going to have a Christmas tree, and he asked his boys if they would be interested in buying this family a tree. The boys gave him a quick and enthusiastic yes, so they went out and bought the family a tree and a tree stand. They took it over to the house and set up the tree. While they stood there admiring their work, one of the boys said, "But there are no lights. We've got to get lights for the tree."

"And ornaments!" somebody added.

So the boys and the houseparents piled back in the car and went to buy lights and a few ornaments with money the boys pitched in. When they had put lights and ornaments on the tree, the boys looked at one another and said, "They can't have a tree without presents." So they went and bought presents. It wasn't easy for the boys to scrape up the money, but they did it. The houseparents pitched in a little, but they thought it would be best to let the boys do most of it themselves. It was such a great experience for the boys that all the other houses started doing the same thing the next year and have been doing it ever since.

Later, I was talking to that first group of boys about what they had done for that needy family and why they had done it. "You see," said one of the boys, "a year ago, that was me at my house."

He hit the nail squarely on the head. In the end, there's only one reason to serve others instead of seeking our own interests, and it is simply this: when we were in need, God sent his Son to die for us and "served us" when we couldn't take care of ourselves. We serve others because God served us first.

Serving others is a habit we all need to practice every day of our lives. Sadly, we have allowed self-centeredness to have too big a hold on the dynamics of our families. The parents of the Proverbs 31 Woman obviously taught her the true joy of having a servant's heart. We should follow suit.

Chapter 8

Stability

 We've talked about seven virtues that your princess needs in order to grow into a queen along the order of the Excellent Woman of Proverbs 31: praiseworthiness, righteousness, initiative, nurture, character, empowerment, and servant-heartedness. But there's one more thing your daughter needs in order for these virtues to truly take root in her life. She needs stability.

We had a young girl brought to us several years ago. As I walked down the hall, I was fifty feet from the room where we were going to meet and I could already smell rank body odor and tobacco smells.

As I turned the corner, I saw a deputy sheriff who had come with the family for the sole purpose of keeping them from fighting with each other during our meeting.

In the middle of the odorous, tumultuous, and violent atmosphere sat a seven-year-old little girl. She looked like a drowned rat. She was battered and bruised beyond description.

After a few minutes, we learned that the grandmother's boyfriend had been sexually abusing this little girl since she was a toddler. Both sides of the family knew it but had done nothing about it. This unstable atmosphere was *all* this little girl knew. To her, this was a normal way of life.

Fast forward to today (nearly twelve years later), she is doing well and flourishing, but at times will recall some event and go into a downward spiral. Her houseparents now have learned what triggers this loss of focus and know how to redirect her. They tell her, "It's not where you came from or what others have done to you. What's important is where *you* want to go. Continue to be stable in all your ways."

Many of the most unstable homes I have known had two parents posing that they had it all together and the fruit in their children's unstable lives revealed the real truth.

On the other side, I've met thousands of single parents whose homes were the epitome of stability because that parent made this attribute such a high priority.

I once had a single mom tell me, "If I can give my kids a stable, loving home, then I've done my job." She was right!

No matter if you are a single parent or you are in the middle of what you feel is the most dysfunctional home there is, let me reassure you there is always hope. There is always a way to build stability in the heart of your little girl. God promised in Jeremiah 29:11 that He has a plan: "'For I know the plans I have for you,' declares the LORD, 'plans to prosper you and not to harm you, plans to give you hope and a future'" (NIV). Trust him!

Remember the girl in chapter 2 who was leaving us to go to a special therapy home to help her over that last hurdle of her moving toward believing she was a princess? She wrote me the following letter, which I asked her permission to share:

> *Dear Mr. John,*
>
> *I just wanted to say thank you for everything that you have done for me. Thank you for taking me into the Ranch. I just wanted to let you know that my seventeenth birthday is coming up. The reason why I am telling you this is because I will be the first one in my family who has not had a baby or been pregnant before the age of seventeen! That is a HUGE achievement for me. I wanted to say that I am going to break the cycle. Thank you for teaching me that lesson.*
>
> *Love,*
>
> *Amanda*

Several weeks after writing this letter, she had an epiphany of the deepest order while talking with her houseparents about her life. She told them, *"God says that he is our best friend and our King. How many people can say that they are best friends with a king?"*

She now understands she can have a real relationship with the Lord and that she is the daughter of the King—a true *princess*! She is doing great because someone convinced her she was a princess.

You *must* be that *someone* for *your* daughter!

Here's the point. To create an atmosphere of stability for our children is to break the kind of cycle that can cause one generation to mistreat the next. This is an unstable world we live in. Our children need to feel that home is a place of stability in the midst of so much insta-

> *Our children need to feel that home is a place of stability in the midst of so much instability.*

bility—a place where they can grow and thrive even if the world around them threatens to tear them down.

And before we get too judgmental about that abusive family, we should look closely at the ways we talk to our daughters and act toward them in ways that are less than fully loving. We can unknowingly damage our daughters' sense of stability. It happens more than you might imagine.

Sometimes we can't see the damage our words do. Even worse, sometimes we refuse to see the damage we unwittingly inflict on our little girls or our boundary-pushing teenagers.

When we don't create a stable environment for our children, they're going to leave. Trust me on that one. I don't mean they're going to leave physically. Their bodies will probably stay put. But they will leave mentally, emotionally, and spiritually.

I once had a hard conversation with a man whose kids had emotionally left him. He was an NFL player, a man whose name you would probably know. I asked him, "How's family life?"

He said, "Man, it's hard. I'm gone all the time, and I never see my kids. After the season, I have to go do all these speaking engagements."

"What do you mean you *have* to do speaking engagements?" I asked.

"Well," he said, "if I'm going to keep my wife and kids in the lifestyle to which they've gotten accustomed, I've got to make more money than I make playing football."

I said, "Tell me this. Which do you think your kids would want more, the stuff they're used to, or having their dad around?"

I thought the answer to that one was going to be obvious. So I was a little surprised when my friend looked down at the ground and his eyes welled up with tears. "They'd rather have the stuff," he said.

That's a hard day, when you realize that your kids would rather have a bunch of stuff than have you. But if you aren't creating stability by being present with your children, both physically and emotionally, you can't be surprised if they leave long before they are physically gone.

The Stability of the Proverbs 31 Woman

There's one detail about the Excellent Woman of Proverbs 31 that I find especially interesting. Verse 21 reads, "She is not afraid of snow for her household, for all her household are clothed in scarlet."

Now, if you're from up north, you might possibly miss some of the significance of this verse. Up north, people know what to do when it snows. The snow plows come out, everybody shovels their driveways, and life goes on as if nothing happened.

But the Excellent Woman of Proverbs 31 didn't live up north. Presumably, she lived in Israel. And in Israel it doesn't snow a lot. Flurries once or twice each winter, and a real snowfall every three or four winters. That sounds almost exactly like the winter climate where we live, in Alabama.

And I can tell you how people in Alabama act when there's snow. The joke is that when there's snow over in

Texas, we shut the state down because we know it might be coming our way. If the weatherman says there's a chance of flurries, everybody jumps in the car and speeds straight to the grocery store to buy up all the bread and milk. If a snowflake actually falls, school is canceled. (I have a theory that kids in northern Alabama get more snow days than kids in northern Minnesota, but I'm not sure.) If it actually snows—not just flurries, but the kind of snow that makes the roads white—it's like the Apocalypse. Cars are strewn in every ditch.

We Alabamans have a lot of great qualities, but handling snow isn't one of them. In a climate like ours (or like the climate of Israel), snow is a destabilizing force. It's one of those unexpected things that the world throws at you every now and then, and you have to decide how you're going to handle it. The Proverbs 31 Woman, obviously, knew how to handle it. She wasn't afraid of snow. Her family was fully prepared.

A few years back it snowed six inches in Alabama. There were 678 wrecks in the city of Birmingham alone in one day. The announcers got on the radio and said, "If you have a wreck, just swap insurance information and go on if you can. The police aren't going to be getting to you any time soon." We were living at the Boys' Ranch at the time, and we had a houseful of kids visiting. We lost power for five days—no electricity, no communication. It could have been a chaotic time. But my wife Tee said, "Here's what we're going to do . . ." She handled it. We had one room with a fireplace, so we used blankets to block it off from the rest of the house and kept warm all day before taking all our blankets to bed with us at night.

Tee just laughed at the snow. Thanks to her stability, those five days, instead of being a disaster, became one of our favorite memories. We got out the four-wheeler, a ski rope, and a trash can lid and pulled all of those kids all over the place. We found out how fast a canoe with six boys can go down a hill. Also, we found out what happens when it hits a tree: a twelve-foot canoe becomes a six-foot canoe.

Life is going to bring storms. That's just a fact of living in a fallen, sin-cursed world. You can't steer clear of every kind of instability. But you can create an environment in which your family is stable and thriving in the midst of instability that swirls around them. That's exactly what your daughter needs from you.

If your daughter experiences stability growing up, she can become the kind of woman who, like the Excellent Woman, is not afraid of snow for her household. She can become a person who smiles at the future.

Inviting Girls into Stability

Every child who comes to Big Oak Ranch comes into my office on his or her first day, and we have a chat. I know I have about ninety seconds to convince that child to trust me—or at least to be open to the possibility of trusting me. These are kids who have been through an earthly hell in its many, many forms. After their years of learning how untrustworthy adults can be, I have ninety seconds of attention span.

If we can't bring stability into our kids' lives, we can't bring much else to them either.

What would you say if you only had ninety seconds to convince an abused and neglected child to trust you? I spend my ninety seconds by making the four promises that are the foundation of everything we do at Big Oak Ranch:

- I love you.
- I will never lie to you.
- I'll stick with you until you're grown.
- There are boundaries; don't cross them.

These four promises, really, are the promises of stability. If we can't bring stability into our kids' lives, we can't bring much else to them either.

Promise #1: I love you.

Hopefully, your kids already know you love them. Hopefully, you're telling them all the time and showing it as well. For the kids who are just arriving at Big Oak Ranch, that's not a given. Not even close. It's news to many of them that a grown-up might just love them without wanting anything from them. I don't expect them to believe it the first time they meet with me, but I do want to be sure they have heard it.

But anybody can say, "I love you." The question is whether or not a girl can believe it when she hears it.

Promise #2: I will never lie to you.

It is absolutely vital that we maintain an environment where every child can believe every word that comes out of every grown-up's mouth. The ability to trust is another thing that has been tragically lacking in these kids' lives. But it's a key part of stability.

After I have told our new resident that I will never lie to her, I turn to her social worker, who is typically in the meeting with us. I ask, "What would happen to you if I ever found out that you had lied to this child?"

Without pausing, without even blinking, the social worker says, "I would get fired."

I've even had Reagan in the room for these meetings. "Reagan," I say, "you're my daughter, and I love you very much. But what would happen if I ever found out that you lied to this child?"

Reagan answers, "Oh, I would lose my job on the spot."

It makes quite an impression on the kids. You can see the wheels turning in their heads: "You mean I'm important? I'm that important?" But it's not just for show. It's completely true. After what these kids have been through, they absolutely have to have the stability of knowing that they can trust anything we tell them. Once I was telling a group of Ranch girls about a trip to the river that we were going to take them on and one of the newer girls said, almost without thinking, "For real?" One of the older girls who had been around a long time got kind of a serious look on her face and said, "No, he's not kidding. He will never lie to you." That's exactly the culture that we jealously guard at Big Oak Ranch.

There are truths, of course, that we don't just volunteer to the girls. We don't say to a girl who's been here since she was a small child, "Oh, did you know your mother was a prostitute and a drug addict?" But anything we tell them is going to be the truth. And any time one of our girls asks an honest question, she gets an honest answer, even if the honest answer is "I don't know," and even if the honest answer is hard to say or hard to hear.

Does your daughter know that you will never lie to her? If not, make that a priority! In order to have the stability she needs, your daughter needs to know that you will never lie to her, whether the truth hurts or not!

Promise #3: I'll stick with you until you're grown.

This is the one thing that our kids at Big Oak Ranch need to know more than anything else: somebody is going to be there for them until they're grown and gone—and even longer than that. Tee and I have been at Big Oak Ranch since the 1970s. We've now seen a couple of generations of kids come through. Talk about stability!

You've seen how damaging it is to kids when a parent goes away—not just Ranch kids, but any kid who has experienced divorce or abandonment. Your kids, like ours at Big Oak, need to know that you are going to stick with them till they're grown.

In the parable of the prodigal son, the father illustrates this concept beautifully. The son went away, but the father stayed. The father wasn't going anywhere, even though his son broke his heart. He seemed to know that his son had to make his own mistakes and learn his own lessons. But then the son "came to his senses," as Jesus put it. And when he went back home, his father saw him from a long way off and ran toward him. That old man hiked up his robe and ran! That's what I mean by sticking with a child until he or she is grown.

Promise #4: There are boundaries; don't cross them.

A few years back, a group of psychologists designed an experiment that showed the importance of boundaries in a child's life. During a school's recess, they had teachers take their classes to a nearby park to play. One group went to a playground in the park that was fenced in. The other group went to a playground that had no fence. The group that had no fence tended to huddle around their teacher, afraid to stray away from her protection. But in the other playground, the one with the fence, kids ran and played and had a great time. They roamed all over their designated area.

There's something counterintuitive about that. You would think that the kids with no fence would range farther and wider. But they didn't. (And if they had, they might have been in danger.) It was the fence that gave kids the freedom to roam in safety. That's what boundaries are for—not to cramp a kid's style, but to give her freedom to enjoy herself in safety.

That's what boundaries are for—not to cramp a kid's style, but to give her freedom to enjoy herself in safety.

The four promises aren't a magic spell. I don't utter them and POOF!

167

Suddenly I've introduced stability into the life of a girl who has experienced terrible instability her whole life. Some girls respond quickly to them, some girls respond slowly to them, and some girls don't really respond at all. That's not the point of the four promises. The four promises are the basis of a culture of stability at Big Oak Ranch. They ensure that we have an environment in which everything we teach at least has a reasonable chance of sticking.

The time when we really see the importance of stability is when our kids go back home for a short visit with their family. When they get back, it's the hardest time for our staff. I'm talking about a weeklong visit or a weekend, or sometimes even a four-hour supervised visit. In that short amount of time, leaving the stability of the Ranch environment for the unpredictability of their family of origin, it is not uncommon for us to have to start over with a kid, building her back up after her family of origin just tears her down. It may sound like I'm exaggerating, but I'm not: I've seen a whole year's worth of work with a kid get totally neutralized by a four-hour supervised visit. That's the power a parent has.

Practical Helps and Suggestions

Like so many of the virtues we have discussed in this book, you have a double goal when it comes to stability.

First you give your daughter a stable environment in which to grow; then, by giving her a stable environment, you equip her to bring stability to those around her. As we've said so often, how did the Proverbs 31 Woman manage to give so much? Because her parents gave the virtue of stability to her.

Create scenarios in which your daughter has the opportunity to bring stability and order to a situation.

Have you ever noticed how a little girl, after sitting in school all day long, will sometimes come home and play school with her stuffed animals? What is that about? That little girl is creating an environment of stability, bringing order out of the chaos of the playroom so that her stuffed animals will find it easier to learn and thrive. It seems to be in their DNA. Meanwhile, boys are jumping bikes and trying to set things on fire!

Consider ways you can apply your daughter's habit of solving problems and creating order to situations that aren't just play, but where something is actually at stake. Maybe you're going on a plane trip. Once you've made it through security, give your daughter her boarding pass and let her lead you to the gate. Show her how to change a tire. Drive her out into the woods somewhere, swap seats with her and put *her* in the driver's seat, and tell her "get us home." The key to this exercise is to have her learn to deal with situations where something is at stake, but you are there to see her through if need be.

Help your daughter be financially stable.

Handling money doesn't come naturally to most people. But if you look through Proverbs 31, you can see that somebody helped that Excellent Woman to understand a thing or two about her finances. Whether your daughter has a job (which I recommend at the appropriate age) or whether her money comes mostly from an allowance, help her know what to do with her money. At Big Oak Ranch, we expect our kids to give 10 percent to God, put 70 percent in savings, and keep 20 percent to spend however they like. Habits like that create stability in an area where young people are notoriously unstable.

Help your daughter be stable in her sexuality.

It's not an easy thing to talk to your daughter about sex, especially if you are the father. But she needs to hear from her parents (including her father) about this extremely important topic. Dads, you need to be talking to your girls about how boys think. They need to be rock-solid on the subject of their sexuality, or things can get very unstable very quickly. When it comes to sex (as well as peer pressure in all its forms), the best definition of stability is to make your choices *before* you find yourself in a heated moment.

Your daughter doesn't need to be making any decisions about her sexual standards when she's alone with a boy. She needs to know who she is long *before* it ever comes to that. And you're the person who needs to help her walk through that process. Prepare her beforehand.

Don't lie to your daughter.

Girls are smart. They know when you're blowing smoke. If you tell your daughter that you're going to be at her ballet recital, be there. And if you forget and don't show up, don't make up a story about something coming up at work that meant you had to stay late and not be there. Tell her the truth. Then tell her it won't happen again. And make sure it doesn't happen again.

> *Nothing is going to bring stability to your daughter's life like a rich prayer life.*

Let your daughter hear you talking to God—about her.

Nothing is going to bring stability to your daughter's life like a rich prayer life. She needs to know that prayer matters to you. And she needs to know that she matters enough to you that you pray about her.

Build your daughter's childlike faith in God by modeling stability.

Your daughter was made to trust. It comes natural to her. Unless and until you do something to break her trust, she trusts you, her parents. And in normal circumstances, it is by learning to trust her parents that a daughter learns to trust God. She needs to see you trusting in the Lord, not consumed by worry or greed or self-protection. If she knows that you trust God to take care of you, she will trust God to take care of her. You can't ask for more stability than that.

A key word here is *abide*, to be still in God's presence for a long time. If you can abide in the Word, abide in the Lord, you can hardly help but create an environment of stability. I love Psalm 37:27: "Depart from evil and do good, so you will abide forever" (NASB). Do you think the Excellent Woman of Proverbs 31 has abided? Well, it's been nearly three thousand years, and we're still talking about her. I'd say she's "abided" pretty well.

A special challenge for dads.

If you're a dad reading this book, I want to give you this challenge: be the daddy who shows his daughter what God looks like. When she looks into your eyes, what does she see? Work? Money? Worry? Porn? . . . *or* . . . Holiness? Gentleness? Kindness? Protection? You're not perfect. You don't have to be. You just have to be a man who wants more than anything to love God and serve him. God loves imperfect daddies.

Conclusion

C. S. Lewis once wrote, "Courage is not simply one of the virtues but the form of every virtue at the testing point, which means at the point of highest reality."[1] You could say something similar about stability. Stability isn't only a virtue, like praiseworthiness or righteousness or initiative. Stability is the environment in which all those things thrive. When you help your daughter grow in all the other virtues, you are helping her grow more stable. And as you create an increasingly stable environment for her, you are making it more likely that she will exhibit all the other virtues that make an Excellent Woman.

> *Stability is the environment in which all those things thrive.*

Creating a stable environment for your daughter—one in which she will thrive and remain close to you—is a matter of safety. Does your daughter feel safe in your home? I'm not just talking about physical safety. Does she feel safe to try new things? To fail? To tell how she feels? Or is she always in danger of being hurt or laughed at, being kicked, metaphorically speaking.

There's an old story about a farmer who had a hound dog who lay on the mud mat at the front door. Every morning on his way out, the farmer gave the dog a kick to make it move. This went on for weeks until finally one day the farmer opened the front door and nearly kicked himself into a pretzel kicking at a dog that wasn't there. "Hmm . . ." the farmer said to himself. "That's strange. I wonder why my dog left. He's never acted that way before." You can only kick a dog so many times before he either bites you or leaves. It doesn't matter how loyal he is.

Our daughters are a little bit like that hound dog. She might not leave you physically, but if you kick her enough times she will leave you emotionally. When her very fragile stability starts to erode, she's gone.

Most of us have caught ourselves speaking in the exact tone of voice, perhaps using the same words that our parents used when we were children—the tone and the words that we swore we would never use with our own children. We swore we would never make our children feel the way our parents made us feel. But we have a way of doing it anyway. We repeat history with our children, who will build the same resentment and bitterness that we felt at their age.

In my experience, the harsh words of parents are the single greatest contributor to the continuing destabilization of our daughters.

Examine your heart: Are there ways that you have been like that old farmer, kicking your daughter, perhaps not even maliciously, but out of habit? Are you already sensing a separation? If your daughter is a teenager, a certain amount of parting is developmentally appropriate; but are you experiencing any separation that goes beyond that?

You can recover. It's not easy, but you can. To reestablish a stable heart and a steadfast spirit in a girl who has been kicked too many times is a miracle on the magnitude of the parting of the Red Sea. But God works miracles all the time, and we've seen many of them at Big Oak Ranch.

When you know you have messed up, you need to 'fess up. Admit how you have been wrong, directly to your daughter. The next step is to ask God to reveal to you how you have been guilty of "kicking" your daughter and ask him to help you catch yourself next time. You will be amazed at how longsuffering your daughter can be if she sees and understands that you are trying to break old habits.

The relationship you pray for and hope for is not completely beyond reach—and especially not God's reach. Ask God to change *you*, not *her*—then change can begin. I promise!

If your daughter has already left the porch or you sense that she is going, ask God for wisdom, a loving heart, a sincere change within you, and another chance with your daughter. At Big Oak Ranch we have seen a lot of girls begin to change when they saw that we genuinely wanted to build for them a stability that their parents had destroyed. Remember, God is the Creator of second chances, for you and for your daughter both. Trust him!

Notes

1. C. S. Lewis, *Screwtape Letters* (1942; rept., New York: HarperCollins, 2001).

Chapter 9

Being Raised as a Princess . . . and Finding Your Own: An Interview with Reagan Croyle Phillips and Brodie Croyle

Editor's Note:

John's now-grown children, Reagan Croyle Phillips and Brodie Croyle, took time to answer questions about the principles found in this book. Reagan discusses being raised as a princess, and Brodie talks about how he learned exactly what to look for in a wife by watching his mother and sister being treated that way.

Reagan and Brodie have such a good rapport with each other. I laughed and I cried during this interview and truly wish we could have enclosed a DVD of the interview. I will do my best to put it into words:

Editor's questions are in **bold**.
Brodie's answers are in regular type.
Reagan's answers are in *italics*.

What are some specific ways that your dad raised you as a princess?

I don't think I realized I was a princess until my brother reminded me of it, whenever I got my way.

Dad was always very much, "I love you the same, but I'm going to raise you differently." He has always said that. I have heard him say that to this day. But that's the way it should be because as a man, you are held to a different standard. You are put in different situations but you are there to protect the princess, and for him that was Reagan. But it's just different types of raising.

Yeah, there are so many thoughts going through my head. First of all, my dad told me I was beautiful every day of my whole entire life. He told me I was beautiful, and he told me that he loved me every single day without fail. And I guess what you hear repeatedly you eventually believe. That makes me sound like I think I'm beautiful, and that's not what I'm saying. But you know what I mean. I feel like as women (for the good, bad, and ugly) we get so much of our self-confidence from the men in our lives. And when the men don't rise to that challenge, I think it affects the women and girls in their lives. I know that as we grow spiritually, we learn to find our confidence in the right things. But until we get to that point, we do get so much of our confidence from the men in our lives. Even from my husband today, that's where I get so much of my confidence, from his faith in me.

A friend and I were talking last week, and she gave me a really great compliment that made me start thinking about the book. She said it's so interesting to me to see your family and to talk to the men in your family. Y'all have such traditional roles for men—men of power, strength, you know these Spartan men, taking care of women, taking care of things—and she said then to meet you and you being raised in that, even though the men are such a dominant force in your family, to meet you and to realize that you are just as dominant in the female form, and to see how that played out in your family is just really interesting. And it made me start to think, that is an amazing compliment, but how did that happen? And I guess growing up at the Boys' Ranch affected a lot of that because Dad was like, "Anything that the boys can do, you can do. If they can ride their bike down the hill into the lake, so can you." And maybe I couldn't always do it, but I did always try. He would always force me to have that confidence in myself. It made me start thinking about that, and it is true. We have such a biblical view of masculinity in our family, which I think in a lot of our culture today causes women to be not as empowered, but the women in our family are very empowered.

Uh-huh!!

But honestly, she said after meeting the men in our family, you would expect to meet mousey women. But that's not the case at all.

I have a working mom friend who feels guilty all of the time. She says she feels like she should quit her job, and I tell her, "Look, the Proverbs 31 Woman worked. She worked herself to death. But you just get it done. It doesn't matter whether you work or don't work, it's taking care of business." Of course, don't look at my kitchen right now. [Laughing.]

Generally speaking, how did your parents (together and separately) instill the princess virtues in you?

The way you live your life speaks way more than the words that you say. Dad used to say that all of the time growing up, and I was like, "Blah, blah, blah." But now as a parent when I hear the snippy tone in my child's voice, I say, "We don't talk that way to people," or I hear what he says and I don't like the way he says it, I realize that's how I talk to people sometimes. So no matter how many times I tell him, "Don't talk that way, don't talk that way," when he hears me talk that way, it negates everything I have said. So, with the princess book that's exactly what I think about these virtues. My mother walked, talked, breathed, lived the Proverbs 31 Woman every day of her life. She is the unsung *hero of Big Oak Ranch completely. She married a man who had no job, no money, 143 acres of land, and five boys. I mean, she walked into being the Proverbs 31 Woman. She washed clothes, she cooked, and she went to work. The first Christmas every kid only got $20 out of her teacher's salary. I mean, she lived it. She breathed it.*

She has told us since before we ever had kids, she said it is the hardest job in the world, and you have to be consistent every single day. And I think that is what Reagan is saying. It's consistency. It's every single day you living it for your kids—and in this sense, your princess. The reason she is what she is, is because my mother is what she is. And with it being the hardest job in the world, it's also the most reward-ing job in the world because I got to see day-in and day-out between my mother and my sister what a godly Proverbs 31 Woman is, and that's what I ended up marrying. So I got to see it on a daily basis, and I got to know exactly what it looked like. I didn't deserve it at the time, and for a long time my wife was the spiritual leader in our family. She was for the first four years of our marriage. And every single night before we went to bed, I would get in bed and she would be sitting there reading her Bible. And every single day she lived it consistently, consistently, consistently. And then, eventually you . . .

You wake up.

Yes, you wake up. And now I see it with her, with my sister, and with all of the boys in our family, it is an awesome thing to see—just the strength, the humility, the sacrifice, but more than anything, the consistency that both of them have every single day. Their children are never going to see them having a bad day. Because, like Reagan just said, as soon as one of the boys sees her having a bad day and giving me a snippy answer or John David then all of a sudden they think it's okay. But both women (my sister and my wife), and my mother they lead by example every day.

That's very sweet by the way. I'll try not to snip at you anymore.

That's really the reason I said that. I want you to read it so maybe you will start being nicer . . .

[Laughing!]

We as moms really do mess up. Like I caught myself the other day yelling at my children telling them to quit yelling, and I was like, what am I doing? But what my mom always did—and I think my mom is the most perfect mom in the world. I really, really fully believe that. Every card I write her includes that my goal is to be just half the mom that she was to me growing up. But what she did is the days that she did mess up (and this is something I learned from her), she would come to us later and say, "Man, I totally butchered that. I handled it the wrong way, I spoke the wrong way, and I said the wrong things. Don't do what I do."

My mom said something to me as an adult that just pierced my heart in so many ways because I think my parents are so amazing. She said, "Promise me that you are going to take the good parts from me. Do your best to take only the good parts. All of the bad parts, shed it! Be better than me." She told me that as an adult, and I think if she had told me that earlier I don't think I would have been able to grasp what she fully meant. But as you get older, you become your mother, the good and the bad. And I think so much the curse of the generations happens. And it's biblical. You see it in our culture; you see it in the church. We are the product of our generational sins. And so when she told me that, and for my mom to be as perfect as she is, for her to be able to look at me and say I'm not perfect, but take my good parts and build on that, and your children are going to build on that, and we can reverse any generational sin that we have in this family. That was one of the turning points in my life. I was just like wow! Okay. So I'm not going to be perfect, but dad gum, I've got a good base to start with.

What are some specific stories you recall about watching Reagan being raised as a princess?

The first story that pops into my mind, as she said earlier that dad always encouraged her, "If a boy can do it, she can do it. And I think for me that also fell into if a boy can wrestle, I can wrestle." So then that turned into, "Well, I'm going to wrestle Brodie because I know I can beat him up."

I'm four years older.

Yes, you are, and I was probably eleven or twelve, somewhere in there, and she had a knack for making me insanely mad.

Yeah, I think I still do . . .

But she just pushed that button, and I was just as mad as I could be—and this was the first time I actually got her. I just picked her up and put her on the ground, and I was about to go off on her . . .

Allegedly.

. . . and Dad was just sitting in his chair watching, and he just goes, "That'll be enough." And from that moment forward, I was never allowed to wrestle with her; I was never allowed to do anything. This goes back to the *manhood* talk now all of a sudden about respecting women.

I was allowed to abuse him until he was old enough to take up for himself, then he couldn't touch me. [Laughing.]

Yes!

That really wasn't that bad of a deal.

Put that down for being a princess!

———————

Your dad talks early in the book about your modeling trip to Milan and how you stood your ground with a stylist. Tell us a little bit about what helped you make that stand.

It was your righteousness. Just say it, your righteousness! Everyone else bends over and walks with a limp, but you stand tall.

Actually, I bend over and walk with a limp right now because of my back problems. [Laughing.]

I hope you put this in the book just like this—that would be awesome!

Seriously, so much of our upbringing was, "Remember who you are, who Christ called you to be."

What is it you tell Cade before every game? Cade rides to every Westbrook football game with me on Friday nights because he is the water boy, and I coach. And before he gets in the car with me every single time, you say . . .

Remember who you are and where you came from.

It's simple. That pretty much covers that answer.

I feel like Mom and Dad did a good job of giving us the foresight that life is not just about what is right in front of you. The decisions you make today don't just affect you for ten minutes, they affect you for a lifetime. I think that's what's amazing about Big Oak, is seeing the decisions they made were bigger than themselves. Does that make sense?

———

Yes, and I understand you saying that now, as an adult, a wife, a mother, but when you made that decision, you were young, right out of college.

Yes, that was when the Internet was just getting to be big—and I remember thinking that every picture I take, my children will see, my future husband will see, and I may have a daughter one day. How am I going to tell her to clothe yourself in modesty when I wasn't willing to do it? Everything in that industry is about, "Look at me, look at me, look at me," and life is not about that. I knew that wasn't for me.

And yes, I did get my highest paying modeling job the next day. That just reinforced God's promise of, "You stand your ground, I'll take care of you."

Can you tell us about punching the twelfth-grade boy in the nose when you were in seventh grade?

[Laughing.] That was actually one of my really good friends, and he is a great, great guy now. But he was picking on one of our boys who was at the Ranch, and I told him to stop and quit picking. I actually told him, "If you don't quit, I'm gonna punch you." He said, "No, you won't." And then he did it again, and I turned around and punched him.

Brodie, how did watching your sister being raised as "the princess" give you a sense of what to look for in a wife?

The morning after Kelli and I told Mom and Dad that we knew we were being called back to the Ranch, it was Easter morning. Dad and I had gone hunting, and when we got back, Mom had put an index card on the kitchen counter. That index card was from my seventh-grade Bible class. And it said at the top, "In twenty years I would like to . . ." and mine said, "I would like to (1) have played professional football, (2) come back and taken over Big Oak Ranch from my Dad, and (3) have married someone who looks and acts like my sister."

Uh, really?

Yes, 100 percent. Mom has the card.

That's sweet!

I mean, seriously every single day she lives it, breathes it, and I have told her recently that she is the best mother I know and has always been that example for me of what to look for. And I married someone who is the perfect combination of my mother and my sister.

That's very sweet.

In what ways did you, and do you, see your dad treating your mom as his queen?

Even last night (side note—we are living with Mom and Dad right now because our home at the Boys' Ranch is not done yet, so me, my wife, my two-year-old son, and our unborn child are all living with Mom and Dad) . . .

Thirty years old and living at home. [Laughing.]

Yes, that's right [laughing] . . . But last night my wife, Kelli, was doing laundry (once again at 8:30 p.m. my pregnant wife was doing laundry, worried about people other than herself)—but she was downstairs, and my dad was rubbing my mom's feet and calves and just watching TV. An hour and fifteen minutes later, she went down to put the clothes in the dryer, and my dad was still sitting on the floor rubbing my mom's feet and legs. That was our whole life. Every single chance that he had to serve her and to praise her and to tell her how awesome she was and to show his appreciation for her, he did.

Yes.

It's hard to do that, though, when the woman isn't doing everything that my mother does. So, for him, for me, for John David (Reagan's husband)—for us and the women we have, the princesses we have, it's simple because all it is, is us saying thank you for them raising studs, for them cooking our meals, for them cleaning, for them taking care of us, for them handling everything they have to handle, and for them being that rock every single day. So, when you ask for one story . . . I can't give you just one story. It honestly is a day-in, day-out act of gratitude.

Do you feel like, even on their worst day (and I don't want to paint the picture that their marriage has been perfect every day because nobody's is, of course)—but even on their worst day, their biggest fight, their worst moment, there was never even a second's doubt in my mind that my dad would lay his life down for my mother. But don't you feel like that gave you such a sense of stability? Like as a child growing up . . .

Oh, without a doubt.

But even in college and beyond, I felt like, I can go try anything, I can go do anything. . . . I didn't have to find my footing. My footing and foundation was there. So then I got to just say, "Okay God, what have you got for me because my footing is right." Unfortunately, with our kids, some of their friends' parents are not living out a biblical marriage in a biblical family.

This world is hard enough with a solid woman at home who is appreciated by her husband, and they happen to be your parents, it is just perfect.

Yes, there is no better gift that you can give your children than to love their other parent, even if you're divorced, because that happens in a lot of situations, there still is no bigger gift you can give your child than to respect the other parent. You may not be married to them anymore or in a relationship with them anymore, and there may be more bitter feelings than I can possibly fathom. But for the sake of your children, I don't think there is any better gift you can give them than to give them the sense of stability that I may be here and she may be there, but we are still your parents.

But I think Christ intended a family to be where children don't have to worry about their father and mother loving one another—it's a given. I feel like at the Ranch, that's what we are trying to do. We are trying to create a biblical view of the family and say, "Here is your footing. Now go tackle what God has for you."

What are you teaching your boys about how to treat girls?

So much of that falls, again, on living by example. And a lot of that depends on the dad, on how to treat a lady. My husband does a fantastic job of that, and I told him that just this morning. The last thing he tells the boys before he leaves to go to work or whenever he leaves the house is, "Take care of your momma." Every day he says that. And this morning I told him you have no idea how much that means to me when you say that. And he said, "Well, I mean it. You're our princess, and we are going to treat mommy like she's our princess." So a lot of that falls on the man to treat their wife and their daughters like they are their princess.

I feel like Brodie is an amazing husband and I feel like he learned that from watching Dad treat Mom and treat me the way he does. I think he learned from watching him. And my father-in-law loves my mother-in-law. She is his favorite person in the world. That's the way John David is. I never doubt that I am his favorite person, and I feel like that is something he learned from his dad.

What are some of the things you see lacking in the girls who first come to the Ranch that reveals that lack of "princess" training in their lives?

I will sob if I really answer this question [tearing up]. It just breaks my heart . . .

I think you pretty much answered it in the *Manhood* book when you said, "How blessed am I that I have three men who would lay down their life for me at the blink of an eye." And it's to the point now where you have six who would lay down their lives for you because I know beyond a shadow of a doubt your three boys would. And how blessed are you . . . but these girls have no clue what that man is.

That's the part that breaks my heart. Here these girls come; they have no concept (most of them) of what it feels like to have a father who would lay down his life for them. I have an earthly father who loves me and shows me the right way, who points me in the direction of Christ, who is stable and always there and gives me such a sense of a foundation. So, how much easier is it for me to grasp the concept that there is a heavenly Father who sent his Son to die for me, who loved me that much? It's still hard for me to fathom that he would lay down his life because of my sin, and I do have that earthly example. We are charged with the task of taking these girls who have no concept of what an earthly father's love is, so how can we explain to them that there is a heavenly Father who loves them?

I think about our housedads and what a calling it is on their lives that they get to try to teach day-in and day-out what that is in the hopes of showing some earthly form of our heavenly Father's love. I feel like the father's role and the man's role in young girls' lives—Christ made that special—there is no doubt that the role of a man in the family is supposed to be an example of how he loves us. It is all throughout Scripture. The man is supposed to lay down his life for his wife and his family. He is supposed to love them the way Christ loved the church. And for us to have these girls who have no concept of stability and all of the things the princess book talks about, it just breaks my heart.

Besides the housedads' role, how do the housemoms change this "I'm not a princess" mentality?

Our housemoms exemplify this book way more than I ever will. My best day is our housemoms' worst day as far as this princess book goes. They are the Proverbs 31 Woman to the "nth" degree. No doubt. Their husbands and all of us should stand at the city gates and proclaim their worthiness. They show our girls day-in and day-out how to walk with the strength and confidence that only comes from Christ, and they show the boys at the Boys' Ranch how you better treat a woman if you want a woman who is worthy of being treated that way.

Any final thoughts?

I would just charge parents the same way I charge myself, just to get your stuff together. There is no time like the present to start living the way you want your kids to live. Your kids are going to have enough distractions and enough things pulling them away from him, so we as parents need to be all we can be to be that stability that points them toward Christ and not exasperate them and push them away. I don't want my kids to miss out on the calling God has on their lives because of something I'm doing. I tell my nine-year-old, "Don't let the days that I'm a bad mother push you away from what Christ has for you." I just don't ever want to be a stumbling block for what Christ has for them.

Live in a manner worthy to lead your children in the right direction. Lead them toward Christ, and don't take one step that is away from him!

Amen!

Epilogue

Every abused or abandoned girl I've ever known has asked the same two questions at one time or another: "What's wrong with me?" and "Why didn't my parents want me?"

Those are sad questions to hear from a girl whose parents have abandoned her. They're even sadder to hear from a girl whose parents are right there, but so clueless that they think they've given their daughter everything she needs. I see it all the time—"good" parents who feel sorry for the kids at Big Oak Ranch, not realizing that they're raising emotional and spiritual orphans in their very own houses.

I don't care how grown-up your daughter seems. I don't care how much she rolls her eyes and sighs when you try to talk to her. She needs your help navigating the world she lives in. Your daughter isn't going to grow into a princess without your involvement.

She doesn't know she's **P**raiseworthy unless you tell her.

She doesn't know how to live **R**ighteously unless you model it for her.

She doesn't know how to show **I**nitiative unless you take the initiative and show her.

She can't **N**urture unless you've nurtured her.

She won't grow in **C**haracter unless you help her see what's truly important.

She won't be **E**mpowered unless you entrust her with power.

She won't have a **S**ervant's heart unless you serve her.

She won't enjoy the benefits of **S**tability unless you give her a stable environment to grow in.

Raising a princess isn't rocket science. It's mostly a matter of paying attention, being intentional, not missing opportunities to teach and affirm. Sometimes parenting feels like driving a car with no brakes and no steering wheel. I get that. Your kids keep getting closer to adulthood and the technology keeps changing and the media keeps getting nastier and their friends keep getting bolder and it feels like the cow is out of the barn already and you'll never get it back in again.

I want to give you some reassurance: the cow's not out of the barn. It's not too late. You still have a choice about how you're going to raise your daughter, every minute of every day. Even when you choose not to choose, when you go on autopilot, that's a choice too (one that will probably steer your car into a ditch).

I like to say that when it comes to your identity, God chooses the noun, and you choose the adjective. God has made you a parent (noun). You choose what kind of parent you're going to be (adjective). An attentive parent? A loving parent? An angry parent? A checked-out parent?

That's your choice.

Maybe you think you've blown it with your kids. Emotional absence or excessive criticism or anger or divorce have wounded your children too deeply for any hope of recovery, you say. I'm going to tell you what I tell kids at the Ranch when they've messed up: God doesn't consult your past in order to determine your future. I'll say it again: You have a choice, every minute of every day.

A parent has to make so many choices and decisions that life gets pretty complicated. I find it extremely helpful to simplify things down to three questions:

1. What has God called you to do?
2. Are you doing it?
3. What is the fruit of questions 1 and 2?

Those three questions are printed on a card that never leaves my desk. As I go through my day making choices big and small, those questions are always there in front of me.

I can't speak about everything God has called you to. But I do know this: if God has given you a daughter, he has called you to give her the virtues of a princess. Are you doing it? What is the fruit?

And I can tell you something else. If you are answering that call, you're going to see fruit not only in your daughter's life, but in your own.

No matter where your daughter is on the path toward "princesshood"—and even if she's off the path—you have a choice, every minute of every day.

Are you going to answer the call?